SIGNED
BY
AUTHOR

'K'11
£4 —

D0231287

ROBIN SMITH

QUEST FOR NUMBER ONE

ROBIN SMITH

QUEST FOR NUMBER ONE

**Robin Smith
and
John Crace**

Foreword by Graham Gooch

 B⬛XTREE

FOR HARRISON AND ANNA

First published in the UK 1993
by BOXTREE LIMITED, Broadwall House,
21 Broadwall, London SE1 9PL

1 3 5 7 9 10 8 6 4 2

1-85283-794 2

Cover Designed by Design 23
Designed and typeset by Design 23
Printed and bound in Great Britain by
BPCC Hazell Books Ltd
Member of BPCC Ltd

A catalogue record for this book is available fron the British Library

CONTENTS

ACKNOWLEDGEMENTS

The authors would like to express their appreciation to all those who have directly and indirectly helped them write this book. Without their knowledge, time, and support it could not have been written.

Special thanks are due to:-

Dr Graham Jones, Mike Brearley, David Gower, Grayson Heath, Brian Mason, Chris Smith, Neil Fairbrother, Kathy Smith, John & Joy Smith, Jill Crace, Denis Bundy, Allan & Rosemary Crace, Terry Blake, Richard English, Scyld Berry, Caroline Taylor-Thomas, and Adrian Sington.

FOREWORD BY GRAHAM GOOCH

Firstly may I say how delighted I am to help in the production of this book. A player trying to pass on his ideas and thoughts on the game of cricket is, I believe, always helpful.

Robin Smith is a batsman I have been involved with at England level ever since he made his debut at Leeds five years ago. That Test was against the West Indies and ever since then Robin has progressed, and made himself into one of Test cricket's premier batsmen. He is a player strong off both front and back foot, with a particular eye for the square cut.

Batting, though, is not all about flashing stroke play. Cricket is a thinking game. A batsman must be able to apply himself to the task in hand, and to adapt to different pitches and conditions. This awareness of and the ability to adjust to a particular situation is of vital importance and has a direct affect on whether a batsman is successful or not. Most competent batsmen can fare well on a true batting wicket, but the test really comes when he is confronted with a spinning or seaming pitch. Runs scored in these conditions often result in the winning of the match, and thus are much more satisfying. The mental approach must be of the right attitude and commitment, and it is the ability to think out the game plan and make the right shot selection that is the hallmark of the top batsmen. The battle between bat and ball comes down to more than playing shots; it requires thought too, and coaches shouldn't overlook this.

Robin has given much to the game. He has delighted crowds around the world, but like others, he is still learning. Robin has not had success in all conditions, but he is a determined fighter and I am convinced he will become even better as the seasons roll by. Motivation he has in abundance, but in my opinion, it takes more than that to succeed. He is a cricketer much liked by his fellow professionals, and a man who is willing to listen and learn.

I'm sure you will be interested to hear Robin's ideas on the art of scoring runs in the middle in the following pages. He has been an example of courage and effort against the world's best bowlers, and I hope he continues to be one long after I've hung up my boots, and I look forward to watching him from the comfort of my armchair. Maybe then I won't have to remind him where he's meant to be fielding.

Good Luck Judgy.

INTRODUCTION

One of the more reassuring sights for English cricket supporters in recent years has been that of Robin Smith walking out to bat. It's not just the Test average nearing 50, nor the 8 hundreds and 20 fifties in 40 Test appearances that provides the comfort, but the manner in which he strides to the wicket. There are the familiar physical characteristics of his shoulders swept back with arms carving circles in the air, and eyes searching heavenwards, but more importantly he exudes a determination that is almost tangible. Robin shows us that he cares. His walk is not the swagger of an Ian Botham or an Allan Lamb in their prime, but of a man who, even if the cricketing gods are not with him that day, will not surrender his wicket without a fight.

Robin's Test career has not been one of unremitting success, even though, injury permitting, he has been included in the England side for every game since his debut against the West Indians in 1988. He suffered from a loss of form early on the tour to Australia in 1990-1 against the left-arm pace of Bruce Reid, and his torment and confusion when confronted by the high-class leg spin of Mushtaq Ahmed was obvious even to the most casual observer. Yet even when he was struggling it seemed inevitable, if not to Robin himself, that a man of his talent and temperament would surmount his troubles fairly quickly. And indeed so it transpired. He made half-centuries in both the fourth and fifth Tests against Australia in 1991, and an unbeaten 84 against the Pakistanis in the final Test at the Oval in 1992.

Clearly Robin could not have achieved his success without an excellent technique. Cricket is an intensely technical game, and no player makes it to first-class status, let alone international level, without a deep grounding in the skills required for the game. For Robin as for most batsmen this meant hours spent in the nets practising the various shots from the forward defensive to the cover drive from a comparatively young age. Yet of greater relevance to his ongoing success and resilience in fighting back from disappointment is his mental strength.

Of all sports cricket makes some of the most extreme psychological demands on its performers. Batting provides the perfect *raison d'être* for a paranoid because they really are all out to get you. You are surrounded by eleven people who are interested solely in your metaphorical, and sometimes actual, demise. As Grayson Heath, Robin's first coach in South Africa, says: 'Batting is a masochistic art; cricket is the only game in the world that is 1 against 11. Virtually all others are 1 on 1. Tennis and squash need no explanation, but even soccer and rugby are essentially 1 against 1, although you do have team mates to help you. A centre might run into the scrum but his colleagues will pile in, and it will eventually average out to a 1 on 1 situation. In cricket, even your batting partner can't really help, and this produces a pressure that is probably unique. Baseball might come close, but that is more of a one hit game, whereas a cricket match can go on for days. A cricketer must be prepared to commit himself for hours on end to a task, and that involves a dedication to a cause that might only be found elsewhere in golf.'

Whilst there are standard ways of playing particular shots, as laid down in the MCC coaching handbook, there is no readily identifiable personality type that performs these tasks successfully. The range of personalities that the game can accommodate is almost limitless. Academic research has shown that personality does not necessarily predict the sort of sport that a person will participate in, nor whether they will be any good at it. Ideally batting should be a fairly introverted experience; a batsman wants to be concentrating on what he is doing, not what a bowler might be saying to him. An introvert is someone who doesn't like that much external attention, but the very act of going to perform in front of 20,000 people immediately puts you on a stage where everyone is looking at you. Batting therefore makes conflicting demands, and each player has to work out the best way of coping.

Mike Brearley takes this point further. 'Certainly you're

expressing a part of your personality when you're batting; your character is shown both in your style as a batsman as well as in your ability. On the other hand it's not the whole of yourself. Someone like Derek Randall comes across to the public as a very chirpy extrovert character. Actually, he's often low, flat and introverted. So it's a bit like going on stage; someone who performs in a particular way builds up a certain aspect of their personality in order to do it. This might be coherent with his personality, or only a part of it, which is a defence or compensation for the other part. A good example would be a depressive comedian like Tony Hancock. On the whole though, batsmen have to build themselves up for the public contest and confrontation, rather than the opposite. So they try and create something that is more forceful, powerful and confident than they might otherwise be.'

What you see of a batsman isn't necessarily what you get. Similarly, one of cricket's more romantic images of the fast bowler full of unbridled aggression is called into question. Certainly pace bowling is a more adrenalin based activity, and is more physically exhausting than batting, but there is no guarantee that the bowlers themselves will be naturally aggressive. Aggression may be an important part of the fast bowler's armoury, but the bowler might well have to adopt a strategy to manufacture the aggression. Some of the world's great fast bowlers like, Dennis Lillee, Malcolm Marshall, and Richard Hadlee, have been aggressive on the field and relatively easy-going off it. In the same way that batsmen need an inner calm combined with aggression, a bowler cannot rely solely on aggression. Unless he has a rational, critical faculty as well, he will be hit all over the park more often than not.

The inevitable conclusion is that players have to adapt their personalities to suit their particular talents, and those that are successful in so doing, providing they have the ability and technique to go with it, are the ones who will achieve at a high level. On first appearances Phil Edmonds may have seemed temperamentally better suited to fast bowling, but his talent lay as a left-arm spinner. He learnt to harness his character to his skill, with only the odd bouncer betraying the dichotomy between the two, and became one of the best bowlers of his kind. Some players will have to adapt themselves less than others to reach a high level of achievement. Robin Smith has found the on-field character of Ian Botham and Allan Lamb remarkably similar to how they are off the field. However, in most cases players will have a recognizable character and style on the surface, but there will also be a complexity underneath that isn't immediately apparent.

Batsmen as disparate as Geoff Boycott, with his attritional, single-minded approach and David Gower, with his more instinctual style, have been accommodated safely, if not always comfortably, in the same side. All players, no matter how different they appear, must have some mental characteristics in common. At the very least they must be confident, highly motivated, have good concentration, and be able to withstand pressure, and the top players are likely to have higher levels of these attributes than ordinary performers. Unfortunately, for anyone looking for a unifying theory for the psychological requirements of a batsman, that is as far as you get. What motivates one player may demotivate another, what builds confidence for one player may not for another, and so on.

As a result, while coaches have always stressed the importance of the psychological side of the game, there has been relatively little attention given to teaching players how to motivate themselves when they are feeling flat, and how to cope with stress, not least because most coaches are not skilled in teaching such subjects. To a large extent players work out a mental approach for themselves. Given the talent that has graced the cricket fields of the world over the last hundred years or so, one could argue that things have worked out fairly well. Yet the question remains. Could the great players have been even greater, and could others have become great players, if the right form of psychological help had been available?

Psychologists generally agree that sport at the highest level is played largely in the mind. Just how much cricket is played in the mind is hard to quantify, as Mike Brearley is the first to admit: 'Natural ability, technique, and mental resilience all contribute, though it's hard to sort out to what degree. You get county players who always do well against sides that don't have quite the best bowling attacks or only make runs in favourable batting conditions. But this may be either a technical or a psychological problem. Some people like Tony Greig and David Gower did better at Test level whereas I always did worse, and I was never sure how much it was to do with the limitations of my ability and technique, which it was to some extent, and how much to do with some sort of anxiety that made me fail to reach my true potential just because it was a Test match.'

Assuming that natural ability, the innate physical and mental limitations, is the basic resource, the coach is left with the technical and the mental to maximize the potential of each player. Grayson Heath contends that if the role of a coach is 80% technical and 20% mental for a teenaged batsman at school, then by the time a player has progressed to first-class cricket, which he will only do if he masters the techniques, the proportions have changed to 20% technical and 80% mental. 'If we acknowledge this, and I don't think many senior players would disagree, then it's the psychological side that requires the practice, yet the majority of the time is spent practising the skills that represent 20% of the game. I think the problems are twofold. We still believe that you need to have been a Test player to be a good coach or to know anything about the game, when all other sports show us that it's not the star that becomes the coach, but the ordinary guy who can actually see, acknowledge, and solve the problem. This tendency might be changing gradually, but the other aspect is that most players don't practise their mental approach, mainly because they don't know what to practise. I'm not sure that I do either, but I think it is an area that will be addressed in the future, and the first players to do so will be the most successful.'

This is not to say that practising the skills is unimportant or a waste of time. Indeed a psychologist with a purely behaviourist approach would assert that it is the very act of repeating skills in the right way that leads to the right mental state. This argument is highly persuasive, for it's not hard to conceive that someone's confidence may be improved by hitting umpteen cover drives in the middle of the bat. Yet the relationship between a technical fault and the mental state of the batsman is not always that straightforward. Is a technical fault causing a mental problem, or is the mental problem causing a technical fault? If it's the latter then no amount of technical practice will solve the problem. Dr Graham Jones, sports psychologist at Loughborough University, continues the debate. 'Causality is always hard to determine, but taking an educated guess I would say that most of the problems originate in the mind. There is very little to distinguish between elite performers at a physical skill level, so a loss of form is likely to be due to mental confusion, pressure, and loss of confidence.' His point is well made if one considers two members of the present England team. Graeme Hick clearly has a problem getting into line against high quality short-pitched bowling in Test matches, yet he can face the same bowlers at county level and score runs. So it seems unlikely that his skill levels could change that much between Test and county games. Likewise, Alec Stewart hasn't suddenly changed from being an ordinary batsman to a top class batsman. The change has been in his mind. He got it into his head how to play Test cricket, and was then able to cut out the flashy shots outside the off-stump.

Given the importance of the mental side of the game, why has cricket been relatively slow to enlist the help of psychologists? Almost all other sports have embraced their use, and the general levels of performance within that sport have improved. The Eastern bloc countries were the first to spot the potential of sports psychologists. While there was a tendency in the West to dismiss every East European success as another victory for the steroid assembly line, what got overlooked was that the use of steroids was carefully combined with a system of mental preparation that was designed to get the athletes to achieve their best performances when it mattered most. The Americans quickly cottoned on to this, and there is now scarcely a baseball or football team that does not have its own psychologist.

Admittedly, this has rather unpleasant connotations of money and *realpolitik*. Yet most sports operate on a far more human level than this. The idea is not the creation of the *ubermensch*, the Arnold Schwarzenegger of the cricket field, but the notion that professional outside help can assist players in achieving their dreams. The English soccer team has a psychologist, Dr John Gardener, who forms part of the management's back up team. In November 1992 Ian Wright, the Arsenal striker, who had never scored for England in six international games, sought John Gardener's help in trying to break his duck. Such a move was welcomed by Graham Taylor, the England manager. Even in sports like squash, which attract less interest, and therefore less money, psychologists have played a part. Lisa Opie worked with Graham Jones for between 6 to 9 months in her successful bid to become the first British woman to win the British Open in 30 years.

There have of course been a number of cricketers who have received help. Bob Willis and Viv Richards received hypnotherapy from Dr Arthur Jackson in Sydney, and only last year David Gower consulted Brian Mason, a specialist in personal motivation. Yet it is far easier to count those who were tortured by the game they loved, and should have received help. Ken Barrington suffered horribly from nervous tension between 1964 and 1967, so much so that he eventually asked to be left out of the England side. Worse still, he was vilified in the press for being a selfish player, as if his mental paralysis was a deliberate contrivance. Mike Brearley believes that Colin Cowdrey would have been an even better player had he not been so constantly anxious and nervous about whether he was doing the right thing. For some, the mental crises become so great that they are forced to retire, as Grayson Heath points out: 'Cricket is littered with players who never made

15

it, and left the game. It's almost definitely because of the pressure, though they would never admit it because few human beings would. It will always be something else like business or family interests.'

It is also not hard to imagine that there are areas not strictly related to on-field performance where a psychologist can help, and which may produce a knock-on effect to achievement on the pitch. You don't have to be Sigmund Freud or Melanie Klein to work out that a person like David Gower, who lost both his parents at a comparatively young age, and who has no other close blood relations, is going to find it difficult to settle comfortably in the highly regimented family atmosphere of a touring party. Yet no one bothered to address this question before the 1990-1 tour to Australia, or to try and reach a workable solution. The result, as everyone well knows, was a falling out between Gower and the management, and one of England's finest batsmen being banished to the wilderness. By the same token, it was less than tactful for Gooch to inform Gower of his omission from the touring party just half an hour before it was publicly announced, and for the England management then to issue conflicting statements as to why he was dropped. Telling someone that they have not been selected is a disagreeable task, but it is part of the captain's responsibilities, and should be handled sensitively. If the captain doesn't know how to handle such a situation, he should be taught to do so by someone who does. As it was he managed, at a stroke, to demotivate Gower, and to unsettle those who were selected with the ensuing furore.

An added pressure that players of today have to face is the increased interest of the media. Almost by definition, any player who feels that he doesn't need a shrink after being ravaged by the tabloid press, needs a shrink. The eighties and nineties have become very much a celebration of the cult of the personality. Whilst this can be extremely financially rewarding, and at times flattering, for a young Test player, it also presents problems. Ian Botham is a classic example of someone who was built up by the press and then attacked because his private life failed to match up to his public image. The public, sponsors, and the media, want their heroes to be a shining example off the field. Yet this completely disregards the fact that it may take a very single-minded, 'awkward' person to reach the level of achievement whereby he becomes a public hero in his particular field. This tendency was noticed and remarked upon by George Orwell as early as 1944 in his review of Salvador Dali's autobiography, *The Secret Life of Salvador Dali*. While Orwell was revolted by Dali's sexual perversions, he could still assert that Dali had 'fifty times more talent than the people who would denounce his morals and jeer at his paintings'. He went on to point out that anyone who liked his work could not believe that Dali was depraved, and that those who thought he was depraved could not believe he was a good artist. The pressure of media scrutiny is intense even for those whose private lives are consistent with their public image. For those for whom there is a gulf between the two, especially young sportsmen unaccustomed to publicity, the advantage of a professional person to talk to is self evident.

So what role should the psychologist take? This is necessarily problematic to define, as the functions of the captain, coach, and manager are in part psychological. An article in the *Daily Telegraph* in September 1992 reported that 'some cricketers are looking for a motivator in the dressing-room, and that Kent are so sold on the concept, that they have appointed Darryl Foster to manage the side for five years'. The need for a cricket team to be well motivated is obvious, but should a professional be brought in from outside to try to supply it? Traditionally, the captain is expected to be the prime source of motivation. Yet the role of the captain has expanded enormously in recent years. Not only is he expected to lead the team from the front by way of personal performances, he must take part in the executive decisions of the club, and also be available to the press and sponsors. Given this work load, and with the inevitable constraints of time, it is unrealistic to assume that a captain will have sufficient opportunity to motivate on a deeper level than a general team talk to boost morale, with the odd one-to-one chat thrown in.

Of course, the captain has the coach to back him up, and to give the players time on an individual basis that he may not be able to spare. Ideally, the captain and the coach will have the same vision, and between them they will be able to communicate what is expected of each player, and show each player how he can reach that level of attainment. However, there are no guarantees. The captain and the coach may be in conflict with one another, may each have their own favourites, in which case there might be more problems than there were in the beginning. Even if they are in accord, the coach may not be any good at teaching the players what is required. The perfect captain and coach do not exist any more than the perfect parents do. There is no doubt that the situation could be improved; the question is whether an outside professional would make things better or worse.

Mike Brearley is wary of the sports motivator who is brought in to get players geed up in a random, imprecise fashion. 'Cricket gives a lot of scope for the mind to work things out, and to fail to do so. People can be helped or hindered in this. To suggest a motivator is to imply that motivation is the task whatever the activity - that there is a thing called motivation. I would say that motivation has to be geared entirely to what you are trying to do. So you wouldn't want a general 'sports motivator' for a cricket team, but someone who was conversant with the game. Having said that, the Australians brought in a motivator in the series we played against them in 1978-9, when we were leading 3-1 going into the Adelaide Test. We all pooh-poohed it, because he was from Australian Rules Football, and we thought, 'What does he know? How much use will he be, how long will his effect last, and how will he cope with the hours of boredom, and with the subtleties of the game? Having said that, we were something like 70-6 at lunch on the first day, so who knows?'

Graham Jones endorses Mike Brearley's scepticism for general sports motivation, and feels the Agincourt style of team talk is of limited value even for body-contact sports. 'I used to play Rugby Union at good club level. The captain of my team always used to insist that, just before we went out on to the pitch, each player got hold of the person next to him and start roughing him up. I was the fly-half and that was the last thing I needed. I wanted to sit quietly, compose myself, and think about the decisions I was going to have to make; I didn't want to go out looking to beat people up. Quite simply, what works for half the team will more than likely be counter-productive for the other half.'

Nevertheless Graham Jones is convinced that the psychologist can play an important role within a cricket team, and that the parameters of his position can be clearly defined. 'The way I generally approach this type of situation is first of all to discuss with the coaches and players exactly what a sports psychologist can and can't do, as there are so many misconceptions about this. Coaches often need reassuring that you will be complementing what they are doing, and that you won't be encroaching on their areas of expertise. I would never claim that I can make someone a better player, but I am confident that I can help to make him better psychologically prepared, and performance will often benefit as a result. The psychologist can act in both educational and problem solving roles. The educational approach might involve working with a squad or an individual on methods of enhancing their ability to handle pressure, or perhaps maintain motivation and concentration. The various strategies might involve relaxation, imagery and goal setting. The difficulty is when you attempt to impose this educational approach on someone who doesn't see the need for it. Most elite performers are very experienced, and they may not want someone like me coming in telling them how they might concentrate or handle pressure better. So often the psychologist might choose to play more of a problem solving role. He would be in the background working along side the physio and the team doctor. In the same way that a player would see a physio for a muscle strain, if he had something that was worrying him he would see the sports psychologist. It needn't be a major problem; someone might just feel that their confidence could do with some improvement. So, the psychologist is available, and the players can see him if they want to, but there's no compulsion.'

One of the psychologist's most vital assets is his confidentiality. The captain, coach, physio, and doctor are all involved in the selection process, which can make it very hard for a player to confide his anxieties, for fear of jeopardising his position in the team. The psychologist should remain apart from selection, though in the past some have been prepared to compromise their ethics. One became involved in the selection for a national team for an Olympic squad by providing information about individual scores and responses to questionnaires. As a result, where it was close between individuals on skill level, those with less desired questionnaire scores failed to make the team. The abuse is apparent. If someone suspects that what they say will be used as part of selection, they will be more likely to distort their responses, thereby rendering the whole process worthless.

Gaining a player's trust can be a long and painstaking process, as Graham Jones points out: 'At the first two meetings the player and I will be getting to know one another – him gaining confidence in me and me in him. I try and get the relationship to a stage where the performer feels he can say anything he wants to me, and me to him, with neither of us taking offence. It won't work unless both of us speak candidly.'

Another benefit some psychologists may have is that he may be trained in counselling skills, and by reading between the lines can pick up on the subtle nuances that a coach might miss. Players might think that their problem lies in a particular area, but on deeper analysis, it might be something else. It's not that players lie, but that their perceptions may not be the same as the psychologist's. For instance, someone might think they have a problem concentrating, when deep down it's motivation, putting the effort in. While the distinction between motivation and concentration may seem rather fine to the layman, it may make all the difference to the cricketer. The psychologist is trained to provide the right mental exercises for concentration training and goal setting; clearly, working on a concentration strategy would not be as effective if it was motivation that was required.

So, if there was a psychologist as part of the management structure, would the players make use of him? Neil Fairbrother reckons that if there had been someone to talk to after his disastrous Test debut it would not have taken him eighteen months to recover from the experience; Robin Smith is equally unequivocal. 'So little separates the best international sides these days that no team can afford not to be firing on all cylinders. I can think of several players in the current England set-up, myself included, who would benefit. Keith Fletcher is an outstanding coach but he hasn't studied the mind, and therefore he might miss things; there's a lot of money in the game now, and an extra £35,000 for a psychologist for the England team shouldn't be unthinkable. Ideally, the county sides should have one, too. Nobody really gives the mental side much thought when they first start playing, but it can make all the difference to having a long, successful career. I first realized how important it was by watching my brother. He was never the most naturally gifted player in the Hampshire side, but he was consistently one of the greatest run-getters; his success was due to his mental discipline. He used to read books like *The Power of Positive Thinking* and *Think and Grow Rich* and formulate strategies for his approach to cricket. It's worked for him outside the game, too. The Chief Executive of the WACA in Perth recently retired, and Chris was chosen from a long list of 85 applicants to replace him. It's one of the top jobs in Australian cricket, and he's the youngest person by twenty years to hold the post. It's not a bad effort for someone who only moved to Australia less than eighteen months ago. Thanks to Chris I've given my mental approach a lot of thought, and it's brought me a lot of success, but I don't think I've got it taped. I've still got a great deal to learn; part of my enthusiasm to do this book was to help me think about my game in new and more productive ways.'

This is not a 'How To' book; it does not provide a course of mental exercises that if followed precisely will ensure batting success. What it does do is to examine all the different psychological areas of batting; it looks at what psychological theory would suggest or predict for given circumstances, and at the experience of various experts. Robin then describes in detail how he copes, or fails to, with each mental challenge. His in-depth deliberation of two international innings from 1992, one a Test, the other a Texaco Trophy, and the India and Sri Lanka tour, in the final three chapters provides a practical illustration of the ideas discussed. It is not a book of answers, but, hopefully, it is a book that raises questions that others can usefully and enjoyably ask themselves.

CHAPTER ONE

BEGINNINGS

Was it inevitable that Robin Smith would become a top batsman? One of the longest running arguments in the psychological canon concerns what factors determine intelligence and personality. It has become known in common parlance as the nature versus nurture debate. Put simply, it centres on whether these qualities or attributes are inherited or learnt. The absolute 'nature' position proposes that everything is inherited, that a child is born with a determined level of intelligence and with a fixed personality, and that anything that happens to a child in what might otherwise be called the formative years is fundamentally irrelevant. At the other end of the spectrum the nurture purist puts forward the idea that a child is a *tabula rasa* - a blank slate, and that however he turns out is exclusively due to sociological and environmental factors. Of course, between these two extreme beliefs, there are any number of more moderate positions encompassing different elements of both arguments.

So, how well does this debate translate to cricket? Is a batsman born or made, or a bit of both? As we have seen, the requirements of a batsman are manifold; natural ability, technique, and mental resilience. At face value, it would seem fairly straightforward to say that natural ability is inherited, and that technique and mental resilience are the learned factors. Yet, is a person's capacity to learn technique determined at birth? Likewise, although mental strength may develop through experience, is there a finite reservoir, given as a child, from which to draw? These questions continue to exercise psychologists in much the same way as the selection of the national Test team exercises English cricket supporters, and with the same amount of passion, too. While everyone believes that his or her opinion is the right one, no one can prove it and there are no conclusive answers.

One problem is measurement. As Mike Brearley points out: 'How do you even quantify natural ability? One way might be to give someone a ball to hit in a game that he's never played before. It would be an interesting experiment to see how much is natural eye for the ball, and how much is learnt and limited to cricket. You could give a cricketer a baseball bat and see how he manages. I suspect you would find a great difference even between top class batsmen. They'd all be able to do something, but some would be far better than others.' Even so Mike Brearley would be the first to concede that this was far from scientific. Is there an exact correlation between the hand to eye co-ordination between any two games? Even if there was you would be hard pressed to prove that this was a natural ability, and not something that had been learnt.

Cricket's dynasties might suggest that batsmanship is an inherited skill. From the Grace brothers to Victor Richardson and Ian and Greg Chappell, from the Gunn family to the Edrich cousins, from Len and Richard Hutton to Colin, Chris, and Graham Cowdrey, from Hanif, Mushtaq, Wazir, and Sadiq Mohammad to Javed Burki and Imran Khan, from Micky and Alec Stewart to Tony and Ian Greig, and not forgetting Chris and Robin Smith, cricketing relations have become part of the folklore of the game. Ian Botham's son Liam will find it difficult to emulate the feats of his father, but judging by performances to date it seems a fair bet that he will give him a good run for his money. Nor are such family ties restricted to the well-known; a glance through the biographies of those currently playing in the first-class game reveal a surprising number of 'sons of' and 'grandsons of'.

It is equally possible that there are so many cricket families just because within them cricket was perceived as a desirable and achievable pursuit, and time and effort was spent giving the right form of encouragement from an early age. Grayson Heath contends that it is this encouragement that is all important. In a cricket coaching booklet he wrote: 'The coach must have a clear vision of perfection. With enthusiasm, he creates an exciting scenario of cricketing excellence around which his little charges may build their dreams. Along the way he needs patience, understanding and compassion as he nurtures them as they strive to turn dreams into reality. But know that when they succeed it was they who listened, they who became dedicated, they who achieved, and it is therefore their success. Be happy that you painted a picture of a goal that they found worthwhile achieving.'

Grayson continues. 'This encouragement, which isn't of the "Ra-Ra" rugby or soccer style, is far more critical than many would care to think, especially coaches who like to believe that their ability to correct faults is the key. I have no doubt about this, for the simple reason that there are a lot of players who have never had much formal coaching. The coach is definitely replaceable; he's an accessory not a necessity, and I think the coach must understand that in case he gets carried away with his own importance. I've an uncomfortable feeling that Christopher and Robin would have made it anyway. All they needed was to be pointed in the right direction – which is why painting the picture is the most significant thing a coach can do. If along the way he can add some skill to the exercise and speed up the process that's an added bonus.

'The opportunity for a little boy to watch a good player and to imitate him should never be underestimated. If you never did any coaching after that, but made sure that he went to matches to watch the top players, if he wants to succeed he will. Whilst coaching I refer constantly to the first-class game. If he plays a fine cover drive, I will compare it with the Jimmy Cook or Barry Richards cover drive, and make him feel that it's the same sort of shot that's being played at Kingsmead, the Wanderers, Lord's, or the Melbourne Cricket Ground. In other words that shot is the requirement of first-class cricket; in a subtle way you thereby introduce the idea that first-class cricket is there for them to play. It's not an impossible dream that is only open to the super-talented, but it is there for them if they are prepared to work hard and dedicate themselves to it. This way cricket becomes demystified from a game played by giants, and the graduation from school to league to first-class cricket becomes almost inevitable.

'I always say: "Give me a boy who is 10 years old, and I'll guarantee that he plays first-class cricket." There are just two requirements. The first is that he has ball sense, and since this applies to 60-70% of the population this is not a major consideration. The second is that he should want to play. If he doesn't he won't have the dedication, the willingness to make sacrifices, and he won't do what is necessary to hone the skills and to undergo the stresses and pressures. So you have to make it desirable, part and parcel of which is reducing the goal to manageable proportions, by showing him that the people who are playing first-class cricket are normal people who wanted to do so badly enough to do all the right things to attain the level of performance to play there.'

Robin's brother Chris backs up Grayson's argument. 'I firmly believe that of all cricketers, about 5%, players like Gooch, Lamb, Gower, Border, Mark Waugh, and Robin, are in a league of their own in terms of talent. About 20% will be markedly worse than everyone else, which leaves 75% with a similar ability. But there will be an extraordinary range of performance between that 75%. The primary reason for that is mental attitude; I guess that I was one of those at the upper level of success in terms of talent, and it was all due to my positivity.'

Of course, there is a world of difference between playing first-class and Test cricket. Whether this difference is technical or mental is irrelevant at this point; it is sufficient to realize that it exists. Was there then anything special about Robin as a child that marked him out not just as a potential Test-class batsman but as an outstanding talent who would become one of the finest batsmen of his generation?

Sport was taken seriously in the Smith household. When Chris was 10 years old, and Robin 5, Chris began to show an aptitude for cricket, and his father, not a person to do thing by halves, decided to find a coach for him. John Smith came upon Grayson

Heath by chance. Grayson was a Natal cricketer and schoolmaster who also played soccer for one of the semi-professional sides in the Natal football league. It just so happened that Grayson's team was run by Chris and Robin's grandfather – Joy's father – Dr. Shearer. As Grayson was the only cricketer John knew, he was asked to give Chris some coaching. To begin with, he was reluctant to accept as he was trying to carve a career for himself outside the teaching profession, and was also fighting to maintain his place in the Natal cricket team. He eventually agreed, and five years later when Robin reached 10, it was his turn for coaching. However, whereas Chris had known next to nothing about the game, Robin had spent the previous five years watching his brother and had picked up some of the basics.

The five year age gap between the two brothers was probably ideal for Robin. Had there just been one or two years age difference, the potential for rivalry and jealousy would have been far greater. As it was they had an extremely good relationship all through their youth, which has been maintained to the present day. Robin respected Chris for being successful from an early age, treated him as a star, and was constantly trying to do as well as him. When Chris first took an interest in cricket, Robin was not slow to join in.

Chris takes up the story. 'We were fairly fortunate in that being brought up in South Africa, we had a large garden where we could put up a net, and a guy who would either put balls in a bowling machine or throw them at us all day. I started at 8 or 9 which was early by anyone's standards; Robin being five years younger was extraordinary. The result of starting so early was that in all his games he was a fantastically prodigious scorer. I remember that I was playing some club cricket in the school holidays when I was 14. It was only 3rd Grade, but Robin was playing in the same match against seniors. He just did everything so much sooner than everyone else. It was clear that having me to watch and copy made it all a lot easier for him. I didn't really have a picture to watch day in and day out in the nets whereas Robin had a picture of me from the age of 5, and he knew what a forward and backward defensive looked like.'

Predicting sporting success is always a doddle in retrospect. You can look back at the childhood careers of top stars and say that their future achievements were inevitable. Yet how many other youngsters had similar successes at the same age and simply disappeared, either because they lost interest or because they failed to develop or capitalize on their talent? There were a few clues early on, but by and large it took time for evidence of Robin's talent to show through. Partly this was due to Christopher being no mean cricketer himself, and partly due to Robin's physical size and strength, which counts for a great deal in schoolboy sports. Robin was always much bigger than his contemporaries. He was a good discus thrower and shot putter. Robin's strength works to his advantage today, as it gets him out of trouble from time to time. If you hit the ball as hard as he does, you're less likely to get caught.

Grayson Heath was initially unsure of how good Robin was. 'When I first started working with Robin, he knew a little about the rudiments of batting and coaching having watched Chris, so he was slightly ahead of his brother at the same age. In fact the first time I ever threw a ball at him, I was faced with him playing a forward defensive. His Dad was aghast when I suggested that Robin should hit the ball as hard as he could. From there on his development was much of a muchness with Chris' for some time. Only after a while did it begin to emerge that he was a more talented player. I never coached square cuts and hooks until they were 15, and so Robin's ability to hook, which in the end differentiated him from Chris, never showed up in those first five years. The hook and cut are natural shots, so we dealt with them later; it was the unnatural vertical and sideways on shots that we worked on first.

'Perhaps the speed with which Robin picked up technique indicated a special talent, though I'm not sure how important that was. Probably the one shot that did set him apart was the flick on the on side that he continues to use prolifically today. He first played it when he was about 13, and I still remember it clearly. I said to him: 'That's OK, but remember that the correct shot is the on drive, with your elbow up following after the ball'. I duly threw him a ball on leg stump, and he dutifully played it correctly and continued to do so for a while. From time to time he would play that little flick of his that zips through mid-wicket and square-leg again; on each occasion I would still say "fine" but would remind him that the on drive was the key shot. It was almost as if he was getting bored playing the correct classic shot and that this was his own invention which it was fun to introduce every now and again.'

By the time Robin reached his mid to late teens, it was clear to Chris that his brother had more ability than he did. 'I didn't have to be particularly clever to work it out, it was staring me in the face. He had torn all my school batting records apart, and had played for the South African schools cricket side at a younger age than I had. He had also broken 30 school athletics records, was a good swimmer, and had played Springboks schools rugby. In fact he was exceptional everywhere but the classroom. After that I always knew that he would be a better batsman than me; he sees the ball so early that he can get himself in the right position. Even when I started playing Test cricket, I knew that Robin would play more Tests than me because he had that extra degree of ability to perform at the highest level. His talent is a natural God given talent. Whereas I have a moderate sporting talent and a shrewd business sense, all Robin's talents came in one sporting basket.'

Even so, it is still an immense, not to say unusual, feat for two brothers to play Test cricket. So what was so special about the Smith family? Perhaps one crucial point is that John and Joy Smith were achievers themselves. Research suggests that this is vitally important be it for cricket or any other field of activity. John ran a profitable leather business, and Joy was a highly successful ballet teacher and choreographer. The fact that the home environment was like this meant that both Chris and Robin understood that achieving was the norm. They were prepared to do whatever was necessary to achieve because they had seen their parents make sacrifices and dedicate themselves to whatever activity they were doing.

However Chris and Robin were temperamentally very different. John was a tremendously dominant father, who was keen for his sons to do well. This led to problems with Chris. He would only do what his father said if he thought there was a good reason. If there was and he understood it, then all was well; if not he would argue. Robin was much more eager to please his father and would do whatever he said. Grayson Heath attributes part of Robin's success to this trait. 'Robin was a typical Virgoan; he was conscientious, prepared to listen, and above all, to do the things he was told to. At some point in learning a skill you've got to listen and be willing to put it into practise. It's often interested me that there are so many youngsters who do things incorrectly. You tell them what to do, they nod their heads, and carry on doing it in essentially the same way, give or take a few minor modifications. Robin listened and did what you suggested literally. I'm not sure whether this was a skill of his or if it involved a kind of blind faith.'

So where does this leave us with the nature versus nurture question? Although it provides a useful and interesting method of looking at the different influences that make up sporting prowess, in the end one may not be able to say any more than that Robin's batsmanship owes something to both. How much to each in particular may be unanswerable. Perhaps a more helpful framework of analysis is to be found in the work of the American psychologist, Abraham Maslow. He proposed that psychological theory had by and large been determined by the study of the neurotic or psychologically 'unwell', and that if you wanted to find out what potential humans have, you should look at those people who have achieved. To this end, he made case studies of famous men and women both dead and alive, and from this concluded a five tier hierarchy of human needs, each of which had to be more or less satisfied before someone could advance to the next stage.

The first level is the basic needs for food, air, water, sleep and sex. The second is for security and comfort. The third is the need to be loved and the feeling of being part of something. The fourth level is the need for someone to have a sense of their own self worth and to be valued by others. The fifth level is the need for an individual to reach his potential. This is the stage of self-realization and is never ending. No person lives his life at just one level; people flit between them depending on circumstances, but those that spend the majority of their time at the highest levels will be those that come nearest to reaching what they are capable of being.

Of course Maslow's work is full of value judgements. It makes assumptions about what is sick and what is well. By studying the famous he equates achievement with fulfilled potential. Is a public figure who has a disastrous private life a fulfilled person? Is Norman Lamont a success for becoming Chancellor of the Exchequer even though he has a poor record of success in the job? Nevertheless, in the more easily quantifiable world of cricket, Maslow is fairly useful.

One can readily see that Robin's home life fulfilled many of the requirements for the first four levels. He had his basic needs met, and had a comfortable and secure existence. He was certainly much loved by his family who are still very close to him, and his sporting success was recognised and respected by his family, coach, and peers. So, by Maslow's standards everything was in place for Robin to fulfil his potential.

What then is required for a batsman to advance to the final stage, and to maintain the previous four levels? For this, we should look at such areas as confidence, preparation, motiva-tion, concentration, anxiety, luck, and social support systems, and it is these issues that we will be dealing with next.

ROBIN'S STORY

I'm not an arrogant person by nature, so it is not surprising that I

31

gave little thought to playing Test cricket as a schoolboy. In as much as I gave my future any consideration at all, I suppose that I was hoping that I would be good enough to play cricket for Natal in the summer and provincial rugby in the winter, at the same time as taking over the family leather business. At that age it's almost impossible to imagine what may be required to reach international standard, let alone to be ranked as one of the best batsmen in the world. In fact it was only shortly before I first played Test cricket that I believed I had the ability to succeed at that level.

As a youngster I was involved in all sorts of other sports as well as cricket. I can't remember idolizing any players or collecting autographs, though today I love it when young kids ask me for mine. It was only as I grew older and I started playing with and against great players like Gordon Greenidge, Viv Richards, and Graeme Pollock, that I began to watch them closely and try to emulate their composure on and off the pitch. I still do it today. Last winter when we were at Lilleshall for pre-tour training I would make a point of standing in the umpire's position whenever Gooch or Gatting were having a net against the spinners. I'm the first to admit that I've got a great deal to learn about spin bowling, and those two are among the best in the game.

To be honest, I enjoyed my rugby more than my cricket, and it was partly by chance that I became a full-time professional cricketer. My brother had joined Glamorgan on a one year contract as one of their overseas players. He had a good season with them, and in the 2nd XI game against Hampshire he nicked a ball to the keeper early on, didn't walk, and was adjudged not out. He was given a lot of abuse by the Hampshire players, but he went on to make 135 in front of the club chairman and coach who were looking for an overseas replacement for Gordon Greenidge and Malcolm Marshall who would miss the 1980 season due to the West Indies tour. Chris was asked to join Hampshire, and he was instrumental in getting me a trial for the club in the following year. So you could say that my career as a professional cricketer in England owes a lot to my brother's refusal to walk.

My father is something of an eccentric. He has so much energy and gets so excited about everything; I've never seen him sit still for more than about five minutes. He was a good athlete and rugby player when he was at school, but he never made it to the very top at any sport, although he would have dearly loved to. He was never much interested in academic achievement, and that's something that has rubbed off on me, because I don't have many qualifications and I'm not the brightest bloke in the world. To some extent I think he was trying to relive his ambitions through me. Between the ages of 9 and 17 my Dad would get me up at 4.30 virtually every morning to train.

In the beginning I sometimes found his enthusiasm a bit of a pressure. My Mum was much softer and I got all the affection I needed from her; she used to have enormous arguments with my Dad about how harsh he was on me for dragging me out in the dark. However my Dad won, and when you're young you don't have too much say against a father who is so strong willed. As my father's eagerness rubbed off on me I began to enjoy these sessions. It's inspiring to have someone who wants you to do well, and I began to think that if he wanted it so much it was probably worth having, and I'd better pull my finger out.

My Dad sounds like a bit of a hard man, and in some respects he is, but he didn't have high expectations for me. What he wanted, and what I would want for my son, was that I should understand that anything one does, one should do it to the best of one's ability and do it properly. That's why he brought in the cricket, rugby, and athletics coaches for me. He wanted to ensure that I reached the limit of my potential in any given field whatever standard that might be, and that he had given me every opportunity to do so. If I genuinely didn't want to do something, my Dad wouldn't have been overly impressed but I don't think he would have forced me to do it. I used to bowl fast up till the age of 11. I was quite big, and I enjoyed it for a couple of seasons. I then developed into a leg spinner, and bowled with some success for three or four years. We had a small mat put down on a leg spinner's length, and I could hit it four times out of six. I even remember taking 9-42 in a school match. Yet when I was 15 I decided I didn't want to bowl any more. It was a combination of laziness and lack of interest. My Dad told me I was making a big mistake, but I thought I knew better, and it's now too late to take it up again. I really regret not having continued with my bowling. Having another skill could liven up a long day in the field, and is more than useful in One Day cricket. It certainly hasn't done Graeme Hick's career any harm.

In some ways I think that my father's philosophy backfired on him. He's obviously proud of what I have achieved, but I suspect that he would have preferred me to take over the family company which his father had founded. The original plan was that I would go straight into the business from school in 1980, and that he could retire at 50. When Hampshire offered me a trial, and thereafter a four year contract, he told me that he was prepared to keep working for another four years, and that after that I would have to decide whether I wanted to play cricket on a full-time basis or if I wanted to go back into the company. At the end of my contract I had made up my mind that I wanted to earn my living playing cricket in England, so he went ahead and sold the company. It shows how much he was prepared to stand by his beliefs and put himself out for me. He delayed his retirement, and sold a business that was precious to him, in order to give me time to discover how good a cricketer I was, and for that I am more than grateful.

All the practice I was doing while still at school involved making sacrifices. Instead of going down to the beach with all the other blokes to swim, surf, or simply lounge around looking at the women, I would be practising. While others were lying in bed in the morning I would be practising. On Friday nights many of my mates were out till 1 in the morning, and I'd have loved to have done that, but I don't think my parents would have let me go regardless of whether I was playing the next day. So I had early nights on Fridays and was generally successful on Saturdays –

certainly more often than those who had been out the night before. Now, I feel more than amply rewarded for any sacrifices I may have made, and I'm glad that I had a father who encouraged me to the point of pushing me. All that hard work has been the foundation for a good technique, which has been one of the main reasons for my consistency at Test and county level. No matter what I do from now on, I've played nearly forty Tests for England, and I've got a good average to show for it. I'd be very disappointed not to go on to better things, but there aren't many people fortunate enough to have achieved what I have so far.

By the age of 14 or 15 I started to appreciate the benefits of all this hard work, and I began to enjoy getting up early to practise. In fact it reached the stage where I had to hassle my Dad to get up, as he had begun to fancy the idea of a bit of a lie in himself. Now I didn't need to be pushed, and I had started to develop the discipline and mental strength that you need to succeed. The fruits of my practice were in my results, as I was head and shoulders above everyone else in everything I did. The point scoring record in rugby was 85; in my last year I scored 217, and the next highest was about 13. At cricket I broke my brother's and Barry Richards' batting records.

In athletics I was entered into nine events in each of my last three years, and I ended up with 26 records. The only record I didn't break was in the discus. It had stood at 58 metres since 1952, and I could only manage about 52. I'd always assumed that this record had been mis-measured in the days when distances were measured in yards, and that they had just tacked on a bit to convert to metric. But then I expect that's exactly what some of the boys at the school think about my records today. My school recently amalgamated with another nearby and they took the best records from each school; even so, some 12 or 13 years on, I still hold about 18 records. My shot put record was 16.70m. The best that they're throwing now is 11.85m, and I bet that they think I used a lighter shot. I put myself under a considerable amount of pressure to break all those records on school sports day, and to do so I needed to be not just physically strong, but mentally tough too. It's an approach that has paid off now, because I know that I'm capable of breaking records, and I never imagine that there is one that is beyond me.

Grayson Heath always used to talk of having a picture of success. As an adolescent I didn't have a particularly sophisticated vision, but I don't suppose many teenagers do. Fast cars, fast women, holidays, a bank manager not phoning you up every 10 minutes – these were the sort of thing that appealed. Sure there was the acclaim as well, but you don't really think about the deeper satisfactions of self-fulfilment and giving enjoyment to others. Even now, without wanting to sound too materialistic, one of the reasons that I work hard is so that I can enjoy the good things in life. It's nice not to have to worry about whether you can afford the next round in the pub. Last October I took my family on holiday to Mauritius, and I was able to choose the holiday that I wanted without having to check the price first.

In some respects my vision of success was realized even as a teenager. My achievements brought me recognition early on. Sport is tremendously important in South African schools. Mine had one of the highest exam pass rates in the country, but academic success was never used to promote the school. The school was always sold to prospective parents on the basis of its top grade rugby and cricket teams. Even the local girls' school would come along on Saturdays to watch our matches, which was a bit of a bonus.

My father used to offer me incentives, and I quickly learnt to equate success with financial gain, and equally quickly I learnt that success only comes through hard work. I was very fortunate to come from a family that was sufficiently well-off to be able to afford such rewards, but I never felt as if I was spoiled, because I had to work immensely hard for whatever I got. I didn't get much pocket money as such, but if I did well my Dad would give me a little bonus, and I appreciated that because it meant that I could afford things that other mates didn't have. He would also dangle carrots in the shape of a new bike or go-kart; he would say: 'If you want it, you know what you have to do to get it.' He wasn't too strict though: if I just missed a target or record and had tried hard, he would give it to me anyway. In my last year at school I was given a brand new car for scoring a certain amount of runs. I'm sure that many of the boys thought 'Look what Daddy's given him now', but I knew that I had repeatedly got up at 4.30 in the morning and I reckoned that I had earned it. Even my trial with Hampshire was held out as an incentive. I'd never been to England before, and my Dad offered to pay for my air ticket, and give me some money towards a holiday if I trained hard for the three months prior to travelling there.

I think that the recognition and rewards helped instil a fighting spirit in me. My father would never let me adopt a 'lie down and die' attitude. If I had a bad rugby game, if I had missed a tackle or looked as if I had let my head drop, I would come home to a severe ticking off. But it was never done in a negative way; he had this knack of giving me a talking to but of encouraging me at the same time, and part of the encouragement came from reminding me of the inducements on offer. I came to relish a challenge, though I'm more careful about which ones I take up these days.

One important advantage I had was to be brought up in South Africa. Cricketers that grow up either there or in Australia seem to develop much quicker. If you took the average age in either of these two sides you would probably find it was four to five years younger than an England side. The climate makes a big difference, because people want to spend the time outside. Who wants to go out and train when it's cold and miserable? Of course it wasn't the same for the black population, and I certainly don't condone apartheid, but I had access to good facilities, and there was plenty of fresh food. Over here I suppose that life was a little tougher, and times a little harder. I didn't want for anything, and I'm sure that's why I developed physically so quickly.

It's self-evident that practising so hard with Grayson and my Dad improved my technique, but I also think that my size helped.

I'm essentially the same shape and weight now as I was when I was 15, give or take a little round the middle. It meant that I could hit the ball as hard as I do today. Indeed I would say that nowadays I don't hit the cover drives and the cuts as well as I did then. What has improved with time is shot selection, and that comes with experience and confidence.

My family have a fine sense of right and wrong, and that was very important to my development. We weren't keen church goers, once a year on Christmas day was all we managed, but we were religious nonetheless. My parents always said, and I believe this too, that you don't need to go to church to have faith in the Good Lord. I ask Him for guidance all the time, no matter if I'm in the car or in the bath. I do believe that there is someone out there who is looking after us. Sometimes I wonder why He does the things He does, but that's life. I try not to ask Him too much for success, but I do try and thank Him for whatever success and opportunities come my way. I often talk to Him when I'm batting, and whenever I reach 50 or a 100 I say a quick thank you. I feel safe in His hands, and I sometimes believe that I can feel an extra strength. When I'm really struggling I'll ask Him to sit on my shoulder, and every single time He's helped me out. I know that I'm no saint; I take Him for granted when things are going well, and revert to Him when I'm up against it. But I don't think He minds. The Good Lord is not punishing, and besides He's been treated far worse than that.

Playing by the rules was very much part of my upbringing, and this sense of fair play was translated to the sports field.

I play the game hard, but I don't cheat. Some people think that if you don't walk, then you're cheating. That's not the way I see it. Sure, if you get a big nick you don't embarrass yourself, but there's nothing wrong with waiting for the umpire's decision. These days there are mistakes, and if you walk and get your fair share of bad decisions it just doesn't balance out in the long run. Bowlers appeal for hopeful LBWs and catches. Is that cheating? I've never seen a bowler call a batsman back if he wins a LBW verdict from a ball missing leg stump. The umpire makes the decisions and you abide by them. If you do get a bad decision, you put your bat under your arm and disappear. You don't hang around for 10 minutes letting everybody know how aggrieved you are before meandering back to the pavilion.

If Dad and Grayson were two sides of the triangle that helped shape my cricketing development, then my brother Chris was the third. I learnt a great deal from all three, but whereas with my Dad the learning came with hard work, and with patience from Grayson, from my brother it came with fun. Initially, the five year age gap between us kept us apart, because I wasn't terribly exciting to be with. Chris started taking cricket reasonably seriously from the age of 10, but I didn't join in that much. He practised with his friends in the garden during the afternoon, and I used to watch, but was basically excluded. Dad didn't push him in the way that he later did with me, but that was simply because he hadn't got the business to such a level that it could run itself, and so he couldn't spare the time.

It wasn't until I was about 10 that Chris started to take an interest in me, and we started playing together. There was some good spirited competition between us but never any rivalry, partly I suspect because in the beginning there was no contest. He was much bigger and more advanced than me, and I constantly had to stretch myself to keep up with everything that he and his mates were doing. A couple of school friends apart, all my friends were his friends, and so I was always mixing with people much older than myself, which may have helped me to mature earlier than I otherwise might.

In time the age gap came to matter less and less. I grew physically bigger, and he came to realize that I was a better batsman. We didn't help one another in a formal coaching sense, but he always encouraged me and was interested in how I did, though of course he was most interested in doing well for himself. There were times when we didn't see very much of one another, such as during his national service and when he went to England to join Glamorgan, and I missed him a great deal.

It was when I joined Chris at Hampshire that he came into his own. He took me under his wing, and was a steadying influence both on and off the field. He was always my biggest fan, giving me confidence when I needed it, and a hard time if I deserved it. If I played a bad shot there was never any room for excuses. In the first year we shared a flat; after that he bought a house and I moved in with him. I'd just left school, didn't know anyone in England, and it would have been easy to go off the rails. I did go a bit wild, but he kept me vaguely on the straight and narrow; he would calm me down and remind me that I was over here to play cricket, that it was the beginning of what could be a great career, and that I shouldn't throw away the opportunities I had been given. He made things so much easier for me. He was quick to point out mistakes that he had made so that I could learn from them without having to repeat them.

Perhaps his biggest gift to me was the awarenesss that there was a lot more to cricket than just having the right shots. When I was about 19 he introduced me to the mental side of the game, by underlining passages in books and giving them to me to read. I was a bit young for it at first. I thought he was making a lot of fuss about nothing, and that I knew better. Unfortunately I didn't, and I still regret that I didn't listen to him properly from the start. However, as time passed I came to realize that there was something more to my brother's success than mere talent. I knew that I had more ability, that I played the short ball better, but I wasn't scoring as many runs at 20 as he was at 25. I had little touches of brilliance here, an innings under pressure there, but I couldn't match him for consistency.

Then I began to take more interest in the build-up to the game, and I noticed that mental attitude played a huge role not just for cricketers, but for sportsmen in general. I remembered reading that Mike Gatting had taken Rudi Webster's *Winning Ways* on tour with him to Australia, and I thought that if it was all right for Gatt it should be good enough for me. I read the book and found it helpful in learning how important it was to be able to control the mind. After this, I became more interested in talking to Chris about it.

Being naturally a bit predisposed towards laziness, the idea of sitting down with a beer and talking about working on my mental approach seemed more attractive than running around the pitch or facing 80mph bouncers. However as I got to know more about it, I took it more seriously. In the end, though it's an easy matter to read books and understand what you ought to be doing with your mind; the hard part is putting the theory into practice.

CHAPTER TWO

CONFIDENCE

Ask any cricketer to name his most treasured quality, and the chances are that it will be confidence. It is all the more cherished because it is such a fickle friend. On one day the game can feel effortless; the ball hits the middle of the bat from the word go, the sun shines, people are smiling, and life is a breeze. On the next, he can be scratching around like a novice, and the game can feel like a sophisticated form of water torture. The only difference is confidence, and at the time it seems as if there is precious little he can do about it.

All international cricketers are likely to have greater confidence levels than ordinary mortals, if for no other reason than they have reached an exceptional standard of achievement. A slight loss of confidence for these elite performers is traumatic because the stakes are so much higher. Losing confidence is part of a vicious circle. If one doubts one's ability before or during an event one won't perform to one's potential; if one doesn't perform to one's potential one will begin to doubt one's ability.

Confidence is defined here as a cricketer's positive perception of his ability to meet the demands of a specific task in a specific situation. Consequently, even a person who seems naturally predisposed to self-confidence, can be unconfident in certain situations. Robin Smith can face a cricket ball with a certain amount of assurance; he knows what he's doing and can generally cope with the problems he's set. Unless he's kept a great deal hidden from the world, it is unlikely that Robin could stroll into a lecture hall and deliver a talk on quantum physics to an array of Oxford dons with any degree of equanimity. Indeed, there would be something wrong with him if he did.

So why is it that the game can feel so simple? The human brain is often described as being split into two halves. The left side controls analysis and logical thought, while the right-hand side is for more intuitive processes. Thus the left-hand side is considered the domain of mathematicians and the right the preserve of artists. Two Swedish psychologists put forward the idea that when a game feels effortless to a performer he has undergone a hemispheric shift from left to right. Instead of getting bogged down with thoughts like 'Am I getting my left foot far enough forward?', the batsman responds to his situation in a more intuitive way.

From an academic standpoint this theory has no real proof, but research conducted by Dr David Collins, of St Mary's College in Twickenham, indicates that there may be a correlation between mental state and performance. He measured brain wave patterns in karate athletes, footballers, and county cricketers by attaching electrodes to their skulls. Those that exhibited high alpha levels, indicating that they were concentrated and focused, but not actively thinking, were significantly more successful. This would seem to be a confirmation of the Zen belief that emptying the mind improves results. What is left unclear is what causes the increase in alpha waves.

Both these theories are helpful in that they provide a scientific metaphor to explain a phenomenon that we all know, but none of us understand. It is not something peculiar to sport. Any creative activity, be it batting or whatever, cannot be precisely predicted. Mike Brearley knew of an actress who had been out shopping and done far too much during the day, and yet had turned on her best performance. She didn't know why; at other times she had prepared properly and it wouldn't click. However, one factor that almost always makes a difference is confidence.

So what makes a confident batsman? Grayson Heath believes that the only way the batsman can counter the 1 against 11 context of the game, is for him to be a little self-centred, selfish even. 'He's got to be the sort of person who can assume responsibility for the team, and thrive on it. If he walks out to bat with his side needing to score 400, he should go out expecting to make all 400 with his partner. To do this, he's got to believe he can do it. I've always worked on the formula that arrogance and humility equals confidence. He's got to be arrogant enough to think that he can score the runs himself, and humble enough to acknowledge that unless he follows the basic rules he's not going to do it. To learn this is to understand the masochistic nature of the game. Once he's accepted this he can work on adopting an attitude that can help him cope. I always suggested to Chris and Robin that when they went out to bat at the weekend that they dedicate the first 50 runs to the weekend before when they probably didn't score too many. The second 50 is for this weekend, and the third 50 is for the next weekend, in case they get a bad decision or play a stupid shot'

'Different players learn this at different rates. Chris' belief in his normal ability was relatively far greater than Robin's questioning of his undoubted talent. Chris was confident that he could handle the pressures and uneven circumstances that prevail when you're batting. Robin is by nature a more humble person, and his problem is not to let that side dominate his batting. Clearly it does sometimes when he lets a ball go outside the off stump that he ought to be playing. That's Robin the humble saying: 'Don't play it in case you get a touch' when he should be allowing Robin the cricketer to say: 'I'll not only play it, but I'll play it well and score runs.' It's a question of attitude. Robin doesn't have to be like this off the pitch. Away from the game he can afford to be quiet doing the things he wants.'

Conventional wisdom would suggest that a batsman would be more confident in a situation where less demands were made on him, either because the bowling was of a lesser standard or because the game was of minor importance. Mike Brearley recalls feeling more confident in a county game after he had been picked for England: 'I remember a Sunday League game in which I played extremely well in scoring 50. I actually felt taller; it was as if now I had been recognized as a Test player I could recognize myself as such.' But Mike Brearley's experience is not the whole picture. For Neil Fairbrother, cricket is all about being in the right frame of mind. 'If I feel good it doesn't bother me who's bowling. If I'm not, then all sorts of worries like 'Am I doing such and such right?' begin to creep in. It's not really about cricket it's about your whole life. When we played Pakistan in the World Cup Final last year I knew that I was going to score runs. I was chirpy in the dressing-room, and I was feeling confident. It doesn't make any difference if it's a County Championship game at Old Trafford or the World Cup Final when I feel like that.'

For most cricketers, confidence is an elusive quality. When they've got it, they're not quite sure how they got it or what they have to do to keep it, and when they haven't they don't precisely know what to do to get it back. Permanent self-confidence is the Grail quest for any cricketer, which is why it is so often referred to in the quasi-mystical terms of an out of body experience. While a batsman should never let go of his vision of perfection, a healthy dose of realism is required if any sanity is to be maintained. Those batsmen that come to terms with the transitory nature of confidence, and have a formula for dealing with it in order to minimize the effect on their game, are the players that will achieve at the highest level.

David Gower has come up with his own method. 'Your moods inevitably affect what you do. You can't get away from your emotions, surroundings, or personal circumstances. I can be a confident or a less confident character. I have to build myself up to come up to scratch. Most days it involves a fairly long conversation inside my head. 'Are we going to do it today? I don't think so. Are you sure? Do you really mean that? No, perhaps I don't.' Gower is sanguine enough to realize that from time to time this method doesn't work. His confidence took a knock after being omitted from the England tour party to India in September 1992, and he had mixed feelings about playing in the final county championship game of the season against Worcestershire. 'Mark Nicholas phoned me to say sorry about the bad news and was I going to be feeling right for the game at the weekend. I told him that I felt a bit up and down, but on the whole I thought I could play. I didn't actually say that I felt hopeless and he could forget all about it! He said: 'What are you going to be saying to yourself when you walk out to bat, it's my job or let's go out there and get some runs? I replied: 'The truth is, when I get up to go out to bat I'll be thinking this is my job, but half way out I'll say now I'm here I might as well get some runs.' In the end I said: 'This isn't really helping you is it. If you want to play Sean Morris that's fine by me, I've got plenty of other things to do.'

Batsmen can lose confidence for all sorts of reasons, but the most common is pressure. Stress is created when a player is confronted with a situation that challenges his capabilities; if a batsman has doubts about his ability to deal with that situation his confidence is weakened. It may be something cricket-related like playing at a higher level, or it may be an inability to pay the mortgage, or the break-up of a relationship. The media has intensified the pressure on Test cricketers, as every action both on and off the field is now liable to become subject to public examination. Any mistake or peccadillo will be picked on immediately and broadcast world-wide, making it more difficult for the player to retain his self-belief.

'Press interest is now greater than ever,' says David Gower. 'Everything you do is analyzed in more detail than when I first started playing. It's not just when you're touring, but the whole year round. We've had as many stories of misdeeds at home as away. Some of my middle career was the worst for that, and it does create pressure. The trick is to realize that much of the interest is made by the media, and not to take everything that is said or written to heart. But you can't always help it. If you see something dreadful about yourself, be it personal or pointed, then it's impossible to ignore it. If it's something that is common or garden criticism, and probably valid anyway, then there's no point in getting upset. Sadly, I've taken that view most of the time, and missed out on numerous opportunities of suing. In the end you have to accept that there are demands on you as an international cricketer, and that whatever you experience as pressure is your pressure, and you can't change that. Fighting the Gulf War might be a more serious kind of pressure, but signing your name is a pressure if you're illiterate. Unfortunately, you tend to feel the pressure most when you're not playing well, and that's when you're liable to come under the scrutiny of the press.'

A loss of confidence will be determined by a batsman's perceptions of what is happening to him. Usually this will correspond to what is actually happening, but it doesn't need to do so. Mike Brearley had several conversations with Mike Gatting during a West Indies series before he got his first Test hundred. 'He was desperately worried about getting LBW either through not playing a shot or by missing a straight ball. What we realized was that he was always imagining the worst because it was a Test match, and that the bowler would bowl his most lethal delivery every ball. If the ball pitches on middle and off the biggest danger is that it swings away late and you get an outside edge. This is what Mike was playing for. Of course if he was playing for that he was going to miss the ball that comes back or holds its own, which is why he kept missing ordinary balls that he had received hundreds of times in county cricket. It was all down to the extra pressure of a Test match.'

The batsman can use this syndrome to his advantage. A batsman that can appreciate that a bowler might be nervous of a confrontation with him, has a great asset. Viv Richards gave off such an aura of self-confidence that many bowlers felt as if he was bigger and further away than he actually was. He could see the confidence drain from them, and his own belief in his invincibility was strengthened. Few batsmen have Viv Richards' levels of self-assurance, but many have found that if they try and act as if they did, their confidence is improved. The bowler is far more likely to go on the defensive if he sees a batsman striding confidently to the wicket, than if he is looking abject. Neil Fairbrother endorses this approach. 'I'm not naturally very self-confident, but you must have confidence in your ability when you go out in the middle. You've got to show the people that you're playing against that you're confident even if you're not. About three years ago I went on an England A tour with Keith Medlycott. About halfway through the tour he came up to me and said that he couldn't believe what I was actually like. The only previous contact that he had had with me was when Surrey played Lancashire. From those encounters he had gained the impression that I was a very arrogant man.'

Some batsmen have found that if they begin by acting as if they had self-belief, they can, with application, transform themselves into positive, confident people. Chris Smith is one of them. 'I wasn't a cocky, arrogant 16-year-old. In fact I was rather quiet and unassuming. When I left school and began to play club cricket, whenever I faced a top state bowler like Mike Procter or Vincent Van Der Bijl I would play the name rather than the delivery and my performances were never as good as they should have been. It became clear to me that I simply wasn't positive enough. Luckily, at about this time, a good friend of mine, Michael Matthews, a Natal B cricketer in the mid seventies, who had made a lot of money as an insurance salesman, was into this positive thinking kick. He told me that he thought I had a problem and he gave me a few tapes and books, one of which was *The Power of Positive Thinking*. I read this thoroughly, underlined 15-20 phrases that I thought were particularly apt, and I found that reciting them to myself before and during an innings gave me some confidence. I read this book three or four times in the first year, and even if I had gone through a period of five games with no significant score I could still artificially stimulate confidence.

'Brain washing yourself isn't easy, but it is possible. You can't suddenly flick through a book when you're feeling low, and expect to switch on the confidence. You've got to be working at it the whole time. I must have read and re-read some fifteen books on sports psychology; I kept them in my cricket bag and would read a paragraph or two when I was in the pavilion. I didn't approach them like novels; I read them slowly, giving myself time to close my eyes and visualize what the author was talking about. Towards the end of my county career I believe that I had mastered positive thinking, and it was reflected in my county scores. In my second and third last years I averaged in the high fifties, while in my last year it was over 60. With the possible exceptions of Graham Gooch, Mike Gatting, and Graeme Hick, I was the most consistent scorer in county cricket. I was so positive every time I went out to bat. I believed that spectators had come to the ground to watch me, and I was simply going to have another day at the office. It wasn't a question of how long I was going to bat for; I put cream on my face, tied a hanky round my neck, and put spare gloves aside, because I knew I was going out there for two and a quarter hours. I would then be coming in for my lunch before going out for a further two and a quarter hours.

'I believe that the weakest part of Robin's game is his inability to create a positive air when he's had a run of low scores. He'll have that outward bouncy 'Yes, yes, I'm OK, I'm feeling good, I'll make runs today' attitude, but I sometimes question how inwardly positive he really is. I used to work regularly on this area with him. He ought to read a lot more of these books and make them part of his life. If he does that and finds a real inner strength, he'll be the best batsman in the world.'

Everyone can learn from Chris Smith's example, though whether everyone can achieve the same degree of mastery over positive thinking must be debatable, as each person has a unique combination of mental resources. Every batsman's experience of confidence will be slightly different. Nevertheless one can draw up some general guidelines to predict what produces confidence. If a batsman has had a run of good scores, he is liable to be confident; likewise, if he has made runs in the past against the bowlers he is facing, or is able to imagine himself doing so. Confidence will also be determined by a batsman's ability to tell himself that he is a good player, and how he perceives what is happening to him physiologically. If he can enjoy the way he is feeling, then so much the better.

Perhaps, in the end, confidence comes down to a matter of control; the more in control of his mind and body that a batsman feels the more confident that he will be. This would also explain why confidence is such a crucial commodity to a batsman, and why his form can deteriorate so rapidly without it. Compared to most other sportsmen a batsman needs to remain controlled over much longer periods of time. To stay in control a batsman must maintain confidence; what he can do about that is the subject of the next six chapters.

ROBIN'S STORY

I think I'm a fairly decent person; I don't swagger around, and I try to be generous with my family and friends. Away from the cricket field I'm shy and placid, and these are the sort of qualities that I find attractive. Most of my close friends are gentle people. However, these aren't attributes that guarantee a successful Test career, and so the Robin Smith that the public sees is not the true me. I've had to work hard at thinking positively to transform myself from a quite humble person into what I'm like in the middle, where I try to be aggressive and dominant. Sometimes it doesn't always work and I retreat into my shell, which is why my results aren't always what they should be.

Cricket means a great deal to me, and it has already given me so much. The only ambition I have outside the game is to be a good family man, a devoted husband and father to Kath and Harrison. I have had some success playing the game, I have made some great friends in the process, and I earn a good living from it. If I'm disappointed about anything it is that my introverted nature means that I don't enjoy my successes as much as I might. I get so low when I fail, that it would be nice to be able to make up for it a little more than I do when things go well. I'm quite modest, and I tend to keep my enjoyment to myself.

To be honest, when I compare myself to players like Graham Gooch and Viv Richards, I realize that I have a lot of mental problems with my game. Graham is just under 40 and Viv just over, and they are playing unbelievably well considering that their reflexes and eyesight are no longer as sharp as five years ago. What stands out with them is their mental conditioning. One point in my favour is that I still have ten years to learn. My brother has been a great help in getting me to think positively, though it's only in the last few years that I have taken it as seriously as I should. I read sections of the books that he has underlined, and when I was playing club cricket in Perth I went on a course that was basically designed for salesmen but thinking positively is the same whatever you are doing. I've come to accept that the mind will believe the information it is fed. Once there is a negative thought you try and remove it with as many positive ideas as possible. However it's all very well saying that; I know what should be done, but doing it and really believing it is a different matter. There are times when I simply don't have the mental strength to tell myself that I can perform at my best.

I was brought up by Grayson Heath to think that confidence is a balance between arrogance and humility. I've never had to work that hard on the humility, but I've had to work at the arrogance, in the way that I compose myself at the crease. Some days there's no work to do; I wake up and I feel 'Today is the day' and more often than not it is. When that happens I pray that we're batting. It happened at the Trent Bridge Test against the Australians, and I don't think I've ever batted better for England. I just felt supremely confident from the moment I woke up; even though we were in some trouble at 1–2 when I came in I played positively right from the start. They had attacking fields so I got full value for my shots, and I cruised to a century in about a session and a half. Curiously enough, the moment I reached 100 I became tentative. I started to think 'Don't throw it away' and I became marooned on 101. I finally got a short ball outside the off stump, and instead of hitting it hard like I had done earlier in the innings, I tried to run it down to third man and I got a gentle outside edge.

There have been the occasional times in county cricket when

I've been too cocky and over-confident for my own good. If I've been lucky enough to get away with a few flashy shots I'll realize what's going on and give myself a talking to; if I've got out that way I'll be furious with myself when I get back to the dressing-room. However more often than not I'll arrive at the ground feeling a little subdued, and it can be just as annoying to get out by showing an average bowler too much respect, which was something that happened a lot in 1992.

Whenever I play well it's due to confidence. Without it my technique goes, and when that happens I don't score as many runs, and I get more anxious. I have to believe that I'm quicker than the ball; when I do believe it I invariably am. I can then trust myself to wait as long as possible for the ball in order to pick up the line, length, and movement. When that belief goes, I either wait too late and don't move my feet at all, leaving myself vulnerable to being bowled, LBW, or caught behind, or to compensate for that I try to eliminate the 'get out' shots by lunging forward and committing myself too early. When I do this my head falls away to cover, I play across my front pad, and I leave myself no defence against any late movement or the short ball.

The way that I feel can often mean more to me than the number of runs I've scored. I've never been too worried about being dismissed for 0, because when I am it usually means that I haven't been at the wicket long enough to feel out of touch. 0 is a failure, and so is 15, so what's the difference? If I've been scratching around for 15, feeling completely out of my depth, my confidence is going to take more of a dent than a quick 0. If I've played two or three good shots and felt good while I was batting for my 15, and then get out to a superb ball, then my confidence won't suffer. I'm not denying that runs matter, but if I'm scoring well then I'm probably feeling confident. I suspect that what marks out the top batsmen is that they can score runs when they are not feeling at their best; in a strange kind of way I get pleasure from doing well when I'm not feeling at my best, because it reminds me that I have the ability to get results.

If it's one of those days when my confidence isn't automatically in place, I try to create it for myself. I will think back to the last game when I made runs and try to get myself to feel the same way. At the crease I will make a conscious effort to tell myself that my feet are feeling light so that I can move to the ball easily; that 22 yards is a long, long way away, and that I will have plenty of time to see the ball. When I talk to myself I have to make myself believe it. If I don't, I'm as good as talking rubbish, and that does happen at times.

Many players say that batting averages don't mean anything to them. Obviously there's no point in having a great average if you've stuffed the side in the process, and likewise an average over a few games is meaningless, but I do feel that a career average tells you something about how good a player is. Various people have said 'Robin Smith is a red ink merchant who plays for the not outs to bump up his average', but I don't feel that's fair. I have had a high proportion of not outs for England, but for much of the time I batted at number 6 so there was always the likelihood that I would run out of partners. I've also been at the crease when declarations or the winning runs were made. If we've needed quick runs I've gone for them, but otherwise I've always taken the view that it's better for the team if I'm batting than if I'm out, and my average does mean something to me. It gives me confidence to know that when I go out to bat, a little caption will come up on the TV saying that I have a Test average of nearly 50. It tells me that I can't be that bad a player.

My self-confidence can be so precarious that it can take just one innings for me to lose it. I began the 1990-1 tour to Australia in sparkling form. In the opening drawn state game against Western Australia I made 98 not out in the second innings as we battled to save the game, and I felt in marvellous touch. Unfortunately, because others needed the practice I had to miss the next match against South Australia and I went into the first Test at Brisbane short of match practice. It's always been very important to me that I get a lot of batting in the middle; it helps me get into a rhythm which in turn gives me confidence. I think the length of time between innings on tour is one of the reasons that my record overseas is so much poorer compared to my record at home. In the first innings I got a yorker from Bruce Reid which I lost over the top of the sightscreen, and for some reason that precipitated a loss of confidence.

Once my confidence had gone the Australian bowlers had the upper hand. I began to imagine that they were bowling better to me than they actually were. They saw that I wasn't going to smack them all over the place so they gained in confidence and started genuinely bowling better to me. It got to the point that when I did get a bad ball I was incapable of scoring off it. It felt as though there were six extra fielders, because I invariably hit the ball to the field. In the 3rd Test at Sydney my lack of confidence showed in my running. I thought that once Gooch and Gower were out that we weren't going to chase the target any more, but Alec Stewart had other ideas. He set off for a run that I would have taken if I was playing well in a tight one day game. As it was I was still so unsure of my batting that I didn't give a thought to a run until I looked up to find Alec five yards from my end.

My confidence began to pick up on that tour when I scored a century against Queensland at Carrara. Ironically, before that game, I was feeling so low that for the first time in my life I was seriously contemplating going to the captain and saying: 'Put me out of my misery.' I didn't want to go through the agony of being dropped. I thought that John Morris was playing better than me and that he deserved the chance. I told myself not to be too proud to admit that I was playing badly; it had happened to Gooch, Lamb, and Botham, and now it was happening to me too. I went into bat in a poor frame of mind and fiddled around for 20 getting dropped once in the process. Then for some reason my confidence and timing returned, and I started blasting the ball. I didn't look back after that, and went on to make decent scores in the last two Tests to redeem my series.

One of the reasons I didn't ask Goochie to drop me was Allan

Lamb. He has been unbelievably supportive to me throughout my career, and has helped give me inspiration and confidence when I haven't been able to find any myself. I told him what I was planning to do, and in his typically confident way, he told me not to be so ridiculous. He said to me: 'You're a top player, and top players don't lose their form overnight. You're bound to come good at some stage. Don't say anything to anyone and get out there and prove you can fight.' I'll never forget my first Test match against the West Indies in 1988. I was so tense as I took guard to Curtly Ambrose. As he began his run-up, Allan, who was at the non-striker's end, stopped him in mid stride, and wandered down the wicket and said to me: 'What's the problem? You look a bit tight. Relax, it's only a game. These guys can't bowl us out, you've faced them hundreds of times before.' He made me feel so good about myself. After I'd square cut Malcolm Marshall for 4 he held play up again to say: 'That was a great shot. Look up at the crowd. There's Kathy, she's loving it.' I couldn't see her and neither could he, but he relaxed me completely, and by the time he had to retire with a pulled hamstring, the West Indians were getting frustrated and we had put on 105 together.

I think there are few batsmen, no matter how good they are, who don't doubt their ability from time to time, though I admit that I doubt my own more than I should. I don't know of any batsman who enjoys going out to bat near the close of play. If the opposing team is eight wickets down with an hour to go till stumps I start hoping that the tailenders won't get out. I don't want them to score runs; I would rather they played and missed than got an edge. I start counting the overs down. 'There's fifteen overs left; there's two overs for the changeover, I'm batting at 4, the nightwatchman will go in with six overs remaining, so there's a maximum of seven overs for me to bat.' I suppose that if I were being utterly positive I would be saying: 'Let's get them out, and put some runs on the board', but I think that attitude is asking a lot of anyone when the best you can hope for is to end with a little not out. Perhaps it's different for opening batsmen since they know that they are likely to be batting at some stage that evening, so it might as well be as early as possible while the light is at its best.

There have been a number of occasions in Test matches when I have found myself praying that I didn't have to bat a second time. Having had a great series against the Australians in 1988, I was bowled by Geoff Lawson for 11 in the first innings of the last Test at the Oval. After I was out I lay down on the physio's bench and watched Gladstone Small fight to save the follow on, hoping that I wouldn't have to go out again as I didn't want to risk spoiling the summer. I thought it might rain, that the Australians might take too long to set a declaration, and that our openers might bat out the match. In the event none of these things happened, and I had to go out and bat for a long time and made 77 not out. It's happened to me again since then, but that innings did show me how negative I could be, and I do now try to think of the good things that can come out of potentially awkward situations.

It took me some time to feel confident at Test level. In my first 9 Tests I played with over 35 different players; there was no sense of permanence about the team, no team spirit to speak of, and it was hard to have any faith that you would be selected for the next Test. It was only after quite a while that I felt confident enough in both my record and the selectors to believe that I would still be picked even after a small run of low scores. I was fortunate in that I didn't have long to wait for my first 50 or 100; it was not only proof that I could succeed at this level, but an insurance policy that I would be picked for the next game.

It was something of a relief to discover after a few games that although the bowling was of a higher standard than county cricket, the bowlers weren't delivering hand grenades and it was possible to score runs. I've always tended to imagine that things were more difficult than they actually are. Driving up to Headingley to make my Test debut I said to Grayson Heath: 'If someone offered me 50 runs now against the might of the West Indies on a bad wicket, I would take it'. He said: 'You can't be serious, you're selling yourself short. You might get a brilliant hundred.' I replied that I might get a pair. He said: 'I promise you that when we drive back down at the end of the game, you'll turn to me and say it wasn't as bad as you thought.' Sure enough on the way home I told Grayson that he had been absolutely right. I had got 49 runs in the game, and didn't think that I could realistically have scored any more. I had received a superb ball from Curtly Ambrose in the first innings, and had been on the wrong end of a debatable LBW decision in the second, but I had never felt as if I couldn't cope.

Part of my self-confidence comes from taking responsibility for myself and the team. I enjoy putting myself under a certain amount of pressure and I generally respond well to it. I don't know whether the reason I've done well has been because I've been able to see the positive side of an unpleasant predicament, or because I hate making a fool of myself, and I become determined not to let myself or my team mates down. It may well be a bit of both, but if I can battle through a tight spot then I'll gain in confidence anyway.

Early on in my Test career I didn't know how to look after myself, and didn't do anyone any favours. In my second Test I was out third ball for 0 in the second innings. We had lost some time to rain, so we were still playing at 6.50 when a wicket fell and I was due to bat. There shouldn't have been any question about a nightwatchman at that time of night, but for some reason Micky Stewart was in two minds about it. He looked at me quizzically and I said I would bat. I didn't want to, but I felt it was the sort of thing that was expected of me as a new player in the side. Graham Gooch looked up in amazement as I came out to join him. I don't blame anyone for this; I should have known how to stand up for myself. The next morning the sun shone, Matthew Maynard and Goochie both made runs on what was a lovely batting strip, and I was sitting in the pavilion feeling devastated.

I now bat in what I consider to be the premier positions for England. Batting at number 4 in a Test match is ideal. In all probability the shine will be off the new ball, I'll be joining a top order batsman at the crease in the knowledge that there are players of the calibre of Graeme Hick or David Gower to come in after me, and the bowlers may well have lost a little of their opening enthusiasm. Likewise batting at 3 in the one-day games gives me the perfect opportunity to build an innings. Again, the shine will most likely be off the ball, but I won't be having to hit the ball to all corners of the ground from the word go. I have had to work hard to secure these positions, and I think I deserve them. They may be the easiest positions in which to bat, but they are also the most important, as they define the pace and character of the team's innings.

When I first started playing for England more often than not I would find myself batting at number 6. Playing for England means so much to me that I would have batted anywhere the skipper wanted me to, and if asked I would move position again, but number 6 is not the position I would have ideally wanted to bat. You walk out knowing that there is only the allrounder and the wicket-keeper before you get to the tail. The bowlers feel that they can see the light at the end of the tunnel, so they start charging in. They have the inspiration of knowing that if they take one more wicket they could run through the rest of the side. Batting with the lower order means that you have to start farming the strike, which is not at all easy. It's hard enough scoring runs as it is without having to see off five balls and then pick up a single. Also, there is the frustration that if it is one of those days when the chemistry is there, then you won't get the full value of it. You don't get the chances to get the big hundreds, and so you'll probably finish with a nice 60 or 70 not out when you feel you could have gone on batting for ever. Occasionally the tail will stay with you such as at Lord's in 1991 when I made 148 not out against the West Indians, but even then I felt I could have batted for much longer if there had been partners to stay with me.

I have to try and react positively to whatever situation I find myself in. I felt as though I was on a hiding to nothing before I went out to bat against the Indians at Lord's in 1990. Goochie was on course for his 333, David Gower had made 40 or so, Allan Lamb had scored a century, England was completely on top, and I was sure that someone was going to fail, and that that someone would be me. But as I walked out to bat I reminded myself to be more responsible and positive about what I was doing. If I had done badly no one would have been saying in years to come that it didn't matter because everyone else had done well; all that anyone would remember about my innings was the runs in the scorebook. So I went out and grafted for my runs. It was far from my most fluent innings, and it went largely unreported; quite rightly everyone focused on Graham's triple hundred. But I didn't mind, because I was pleased that I had shown the resolve and confidence to make a success of an unpromising start to an innings.

I feel that this is an approach that Graeme Hick should have taken last year when he was pushed down the order from 3 to 7 for the Headingley Test. I know that he wasn't keen about it, but in some ways he was lucky to get the opportunity. He had been given a lot of chances at 3 and rightly so because he's a special player, but he had only made one half century, so it was either 7 or nowhere. To give him credit he didn't mope around the dressing-room, but I don't think he had considered how to use his situation positively. He should have thought about how the 30 or 40 that he could have made on that wicket was worth 70 or 80 in another position on another ground.

In many ways pressure is relative. I now find county cricket a little easier than I once did, but then I would have hoped that would be the case after 10 years as a professional. I've become a better player so the bowling doesn't always seem as threatening. I can relax in the dressing-room, and hopefully, especially at big games like the Nat West and Benson and Hedges finals, the younger players can draw confidence from my attitude.

Test cricket is another matter. Obviously I'm more confident of my ability to handle the stresses than I was when I first played, but I also feel that Test players need more self-belief nowadays than before because the pressures at that level have grown. After I had played seven or eight Tests I can remember asking David Gower how he had managed to play 100 Tests without cracking up. He replied that international cricket had changed in character since his debut, and that he would seriously doubt his ability to play 100 Tests with his sanity intact if he was playing his first Test now. There's more money in the game, so there has to be more commitment. More is asked of you; sponsors want something in return for their money, and it's called success. Likewise sport in general has become much more of a symbol of a nation's virility. Politicians want to be seen to be involved, and in a recession success can lift people's spirits and give them something to cheer for. Cricket is no exception to this, and the pressure on the players can be intense.

The pressure is fuelled by the media. I understand that the papers must have a story, so I've always tried to take the view that I would rather tell a reporter the truth than have him make something up. I do think it would be much better if they could be a little slower to use superlatives about the players when they do well and a little slower to criticize when things go badly, but I realize that this is not the way to sell a paper. I've been lucky so far in that I haven't really suffered at the hands of the press like some players have, and I hope I never do. I generally know when I'm going to be criticized in the press, and ideally I wouldn't bother to read it, but it can be hard not to. Having said that, provided that the criticism isn't just spiteful or vindictive, you can learn from what other people say and use it to your advantage. The press were generally fair about my performances on the 1990-1 Australia tour, but they were nonetheless reported as disappointing overall. I realized that this assessment must mean that the press held me in high regard since there were a number of players who averaged a lot less than me in that series about whom little was said. The figures are etched on my mind. I averaged just under 30, while Steve Waugh managed 18, Dean Jones 21, Mike Atherton 27, and Allan Lamb 27. So in a way I am proud that an average of 30 should be regarded as failure.

Accepting that I'm going to fail from time to time, and being able to maintain some self-belief that I am a good cricketer and that success will come again, are the things that I find so difficult, and I'm sure that many other cricketers do too. 1992 is the perfect example of a year which began and ended with me feeling supremely confident but which plumbed the depths of despair in between. I'm normally quite a light-hearted, bouncy, jokey character, but in my worst moments I became overcome with lethargy, became ratty with Kath, and the Hampshire players noticed that I had become withdrawn and sarcastic.

I had felt in good touch on the New Zealand leg of the winter tour; my timing was good, I was batting instinctively rather than analytically, and I was looking forward to a successful World Cup. Our first game was in Perth where I played a useful innings of 91, but then a combination of events took over. Our bowlers began to do so well that for the next three games there was little for the batsmen to do, and what with being run out while batting with Ian Botham, and playing a couple of loose shots, I began to lose my rhythm. I have always had an indifferent record against the white ball, and I now began to question my ability to pick it as early as the red ball, and the net result was I began to lose confidence.

I became even more depressed when I injured myself in practice before the semi-final. I had played about 60 consecutive games for England without injury or being dropped, and I was going to have to miss England's most important one-day game for four years, and against South Africa at that. I made myself available for the final. Goochie knew how much I wanted to play, but he was very honest with me and said that I wasn't playing as well as he or I would have liked and that I wasn't going to be included in the final XI. I appreciated Graham's honesty in explaining his decision, but about ten minutes later Micky Stewart told me that I was being left out because they couldn't be sure of my fitness. I was never too sure why I didn't play in the final. Maybe it was a mixture of form and fitness, but in my mind it was a vote of no confidence because I had said that I was fit and had not been selected.

When I got home I felt that I had to approach the situation as if I had to regain my England place, because as far as I was concerned I hadn't made the last team to play for England. In some ways this negative attitude proved an inspiration to me, because although I was jaded after the World Cup, I wanted to score runs early in the season to win back my place. I wasn't trying to get back at Goochie, but I wanted to let him know that the decision not to play me in the final was not the best he had ever made. My early season form for Hampshire was good enough to get me picked for the first one-day game against Pakistan at Lord's, and if I wasn't brimming with confidence, I was determined that I wasn't going to give my wicket away against the opponents who had beaten us in the World Cup final.

I didn't play particularly well early on, but I made sure that I picked up the ones and twos. Gradually my confidence increased up and I went on to score 87. Even so I was never totally happy against Mushtaq, though there was no reason why I should have been as I had never faced a top class leg-spinner before. We had one confrontation at Lord's when I failed to pick the googly and he said: 'You won't get away with that in the Test matches.' The next ball he dropped it short and I pulled him to deep mid-wicket for a single, and as I ran past him I told him that in a Test match it would have been four. It was nice to get my own back; but, although I was pleased with the outcome at Lord's, I knew that Mushtaq was going to give me a lot of trouble throughout the summer.

A low score at the Oval in the second Texaco game was followed by a century at Edgbaston. It's always an achievement to make a Test hundred, but I knew that Mushtaq had not been at his best and that nonetheless I had been fairly fortunate against him. I realized that batting at 4 meant that I would have to face a great deal of Mushtaq in the remaining games, and that if I was going to survive and make runs, I needed a plan to compensate for my inability to pick him. I decided to move my guard to middle and off. The idea was that even if he bowled a googly it wouldn't matter that I couldn't read it since I would be able to get my front pad far enough outside the off stump to rule out the possibility of an LBW decision. The more I thought about this theory the more I liked it and I went to Lord's expecting to make a decent score. However, Mushtaq was more intelligent than I gave him credit for; he saw that I had come over to the off side, so he began to attack my leg stump and before long I was bowled round my legs.

After this I began to get fairly depressed, because I didn't know what to do to counteract him. Everything started to get on top of me; the way the Pakistanis played their cricket, with the non-stop sledging, got to me, and I couldn't stop thinking about them even when I was at home trying to relax in front of the TV. I completely lost my sense of perspective, and my sense of humour went with it. If I had been in a better mental state I would have been able to laugh off some of the more bizarre antics of the Pakistanis, but they had got under my skin and what's more they knew it, which meant that their tactics had paid off.

By the time we played the third Test at Old Trafford I was in poor shape, and the way that I got out was indicative of this. I didn't move my feet and I was stuck in no-man's land when Aqib trapped me leg before. It was a quickish wicket so I wasn't looking to get too far forward, but Aqib didn't have the pace to bounce me out and to play that sort of shot to a bowler of his speed was extremely worrying. This was the low point of the summer. I wasn't in the slightest bit disappointed to have just one innings. In fact I was counting on it, because given the way I was feeling, if I had had to bat again I don't think I would have lasted too long.

The turning point came when we played Glamorgan at Portsmouth. Portsmouth has never been my favourite ground, and I wasn't looking forward to our two fixtures there with any great pleasure, but meeting up with Viv Richards proved to be inspirational. At the end of the first day's play he asked me if I had time to have a drink with him. I was delighted, but we never got round to it, so on the last day he approached me again and said:

'Don't shoot off afterwards, let's have a chat', and he was the one who had to drive back to Glamorgan. He sat me down in the dressing-room and said: 'What's wrong? Stop looking so sorry for yourself.' He went on to say that he had always remembered me walking in with my head held high, but now I was looking beaten before I started. He told me to stop worrying about the Pakistanis and to focus on my own abilities. Knowing that someone whom I admired so much had taken the time to watch me that closely and wanted me to do well was just the boost I needed.

I then began to work seriously on thinking positively about my game. I even had a new haircut as a symbol of this change of attitude. I took my renewed confidence to Lord's for the Benson and Hedges final. My runs there confirmed to me that I hadn't lost it, and I was feeling much better about myself as the fourth Test began. In fact the way that I got out in the first innings was a sign of over-confidence if anything, as I tried to smash a wide ball through the covers. 44 wasn't a huge score but on a poor Headingley surface and given my poor run of scores it felt like a good rehabilitation.

I was out to a nervous shot in the second innings as I jabbed Waqar, my arch-rival, to short mid-wicket, which was upsetting, but with only one Test to go I could see the light at the end of the series. I knew that even if I didn't do well at the Oval I would still be averaging 30 for the series, and Goochie had already told me that I would be going on the tour to India. I still hadn't worked out Mushtaq, and even though I batted for a long time in the first innings when he bowled me with a googly that turned out of Wasim's footmarks, I felt I was back to square one. It was during the tea interval that Goochie told me to watch him through the air and play him from the crease. Other people had said this to me before, but I hadn't wanted to do it because I didn't know which way it was going to spin, and if I didn't use my feet I couldn't see how I was going to score any runs against him unless he dropped the ball short. However I now decided to try this tactic. Although I couldn't pick the ball in the air I played every ball as if it was the

64

wrong'un and concluded that it didn't matter if I couldn't score against him, because with any luck I could get my runs against Wasim and Waqar. This is exactly what happened; I still couldn't pick him, I couldn't score off him, but it didn't matter, and I ended the series with 84 not out.

My confidence was now sky high; I was so positive about my cricket that I was even able to work out a plan for the remaining Texaco games that meant that I would be able to score off Mushtaq. If I decided to sweep I could still score despite playing from the crease, and the matches at Trent Bridge and Old Trafford proved my theory right. 1992 was a difficult year, but I have learnt from it. I know that I can come though the troughs, and that there is a great deal more I can learn about thinking positively. Even though my ability to control my mind and retain my self-confidence has markedly improved over the last few years, I'm still very much a beginner on that front.

CHAPTER THREE

PREPARATION

The batsman's role is essentially reactive. He can be aggressively or negatively reactive, but his choice of shot will by and large be determined by the type of ball bowled, and by the field set by the opposing captain. So, the batsman has to prepare for the unknown. Cricket appears to follow a set pattern; as the bowler runs in, the batsman takes guard, the wicket-keeper and slips crouch down behind the stumps, and the out-fielders walk in from their positions. But there the order and the certainty ends. Each delivery will be different, if only slightly, from any other. It will vary in pace, line, length, bounce, and movement, and each pitch will have its own peculiarities depending on the weather, the soil, and the wear and tear of the surface. As if this wasn't bad enough the batsman has to be ready to take on this uncertainty for hours on end.

Given the mental demands of preparing to control the unknown, many batsmen adopt a form of ritualized behaviour both before they go out to bat and whilst waiting to receive the ball at the crease. The more familiar that a situation becomes, the more comfortable and confident a batsman will feel. One way of making a situation familiar is to seek to impose some control over it. A batsman may well adopt some mannerism at the wicket to remind himself that he isn't at the mercy of the opposition and that he has some say in the proceedings. Chris Tavare always used to go for a little walkabout, whilst Geoff Boycott would always adjust his box. Performing a particular act can often trigger a chain of thought, and providing that the right positive messages are being sent to the brain, it doesn't matter whether such acts are rational or neurotic.

Each batsman will try to find a way of preparing that is suitable for him. A basic level of physical fitness is vital, as is a certain amount of technical practice in the nets so that the batsman can familiarize himself with the type of bowling he will face in the middle, but even the coaching manuals admit that batting is an imperfect science. It is taught around general principles of horizontal and vertical strokes but nothing is ever guaranteed. This ensures that adequate mental preparation is all the more important, as David Gower points out. 'At the end of each season if you go back over your bad days you will often find that the times you got out early in an innings were when you started to play without having got mentally ready for it. You might have thought you were ready at the time, but you weren't. It doesn't necessarily matter whether you click into gear as you are walking out to bat, or whether it's ten minutes or two hours beforehand, as long as you do. It's far from ideal to leave it to the last moment, because you really want to be on top of your will to succeed before you put your whites on. Asking the outgoing batsman en route to the wicket who got him out can be rather disconcerting if the answer is Allan Donald.'

Everything that a batsman does is syntonic with his personality. The way that he stands at the wicket will tell a trained observer something about his character. Graham Gooch looks determined, but the fact that he holds his bat in the air suggests that he is willing to do things in his own way. The Pakistani batsman, Shoaib Mohammad, has a cramped, crab-like stance that almost precludes stroke play and gives more than a hint of his reserved, quiet nature. Some parts of a player's personality may well be in conflict with other parts on the cricket field, but everybody's unique psychological profile means that there can be no one method of preparation that brings everyone to their peak of mental readiness, a point that Mike Brearley acknowledged when he was captain of England and Middlesex. 'Geoff Boycott would always feel better if he had been batting regularly and rhythmically over the previous couple of days. In other words he wanted all the practice he could get. If he got this he would feel that his body was in harmony, and that he had done his duty to himself. So for him to have a few nets in the days leading up to a Test match, an extra net on the afternoon before, and one on the morning, was his rhythm of preparation and made it more likely that he would respond the right way in the middle. To put Botham or Gower in the nets this long before a Test would be a disaster. If Botham was playing all right and didn't want a net that was fine by me. When Fred Titmus was bowling well he didn't want a net. He'd do an over or two, but he didn't want an hour's practice because he'd probably bowled 25–30 overs the day before. But if he wasn't feeling right he would go to a net, preferably without a batsman, and with a stump lined up on a length outside the off stump he'd carry on bowling till he felt he was back in rhythm. On one tour he took six wickets in an innings, despite having 4 or 5 catches dropped off his bowling, but the next morning he was in the nets while we were batting because he didn't feel right.'

Of course, this does not mean that a batsman will necessarily know how best to prepare himself, and that he cannot get it wrong. Neil Fairbrother freely admits that he initially failed to work out that what was required of him at Test level was different to what was needed in a county game or a one-day international, and so he never made the adjustments in his preparation. 'I've tended to approach every day of every game in much the same manner, and I didn't come to terms with the different demands of Test cricket as soon as I should have done. I've always played in a particular way which I haven't wanted to change because I enjoy doing it, but I have to face up to the fact that I took the way I play into Test cricket and it didn't work. I got my second chance at Test level in 1990 against the New Zealanders after scoring plenty of runs in my attacking style for Lancashire. I tried to adopt a more restrained approach for the first Test and batted for a long time for about 20. As I walked off I thought to myself that if I had stayed in for that long playing the way I did for Lancashire I would have made 50 or 60, so I decided to be more aggressive for the next Test. At Lord's I got off the mark, and then tried to clout Bracewell over the top and holed out to mid-on with a shot that wouldn't have been out of place in a farmer's XI. Two low scores in the next game put an end to that part of my career, and the truth is that I hadn't worked out a balanced game plan to cope with Test cricket. Everyone has their own ideas of what you should or shouldn't be doing, but it's something that you have to work out for yourself. I think I have a much better idea now; I just hope it's not too late for me to prove it.'

Neil Fairbrother suspects that there may have been a more fundamental flaw in his preparation over and above failing to work out a plan to cope with Test cricket. 'If I'm not feeling in the right mood, I will try all sorts of things to get me into it. I'll often try to build myself up with aggression to get the adrenalin going, but perhaps that's not the right way to go about it.' There's nothing wrong with aggression per se as a tool of mental preparation, except that Fairbrother identifies feeling relaxed as his ideal mental state for batting. Getting worked up is a fairly topsy-turvy way of getting relaxed, and perhaps he would be better off learning how to relax and feed himself positive messages. Of course, this is a logical solution, and the mind does not always conform to logical patterns. Neil Fairbrother must reach a method with which he is happy, but the fact that he is at present uncertain of what is right indicates that the logical way may be worth a try.

Part of any player's mental preparation will be to feel comfortable with any somatic (physical) symptoms that he is experiencing. Batting is a stressful ordeal, and most batsmen will undergo physical signs of stress; the important thing is that such symptoms are recognized as an integral part of the preparation period. Physical symptoms may range from butterflies in the stomach to, in extreme cases, being sick. It is said that Frank Hayes, the Lancashire and England batsman, was always physically sick before a major innings. Most people would be horrified at the idea of being sick before batting, and would take it as a sign that something had gone badly wrong with their preparation. Yet it does not have to be viewed like this. There was an international footballer who was almost always sick before a big game, and he would only get worried if he wasn't. Vomiting was an indication to him that he was in the right mental state to give of his best. Being sick is not recommended, but it does show that there is no physical state that cannot be incorporated into a preparation programme if the right mental processes are used.

So what tools can a batsman use to prepare himself psychologically? We have already touched on relaxation, but visualization, the creation of positive mental images, is another method that has been very successful for many batsmen. Grayson Heath stumbled across it for himself without realizing it was standard psychology. 'It was during my second year at university, when I didn't have too many early lectures, and my work load was lighter than in my first year. I would think of the upcoming match at the weekend and I would play the innings through in my head. I would work out who the bowlers were likely to be, what sort of pitch we would be playing on, and I would visualize myself facing each bowler in turn. I would imagine the innings in both sunny and overcast conditions, and I would see myself facing the bowlers' complete repertoire of both good and bad balls and playing with confidence. I would do this at all sorts of times; on my motorbike, in the car, or even on the toilet. I didn't realize what I was doing; I was just an enthusiast who preferred cricket to lectures, and wanted to do well at it. I don't think it was coincidental that I had one of my best seasons that year. I've often thought about it since, and I realize that it was a wonderful preparation. I was giving myself all the alternatives for the weekend game, and when I walked out to the middle it was in some way familiar.'

Grayson Heath's experience rubbed off on Chris Smith who in turn formulated a highly structured plan of preparation. Central to Chris' preparation was long net sessions. In his early days at Hampshire he found that he had carte blanche to use the bowling machine because no one else was that interested in practising outside formal net sessions. His dedication and results gradually made an impression on his colleagues, and by the end of his career he found it increasingly difficult to get all the practice he wanted, as queues had begun to form for the bowling machines. 'Each innings was a big deal, and I wasn't going to give it away through inattention to detail. Every morning I would have a net when I got to the ground. If our opponents had a left-armer and we didn't I would get our bowlers to go round the wicket so that I could get used to the line. I would know what guard I would be taking against each bowler, and where he would be probing me. The short pitched ball wasn't a huge strength of mine, but I would always make sure the bowlers would give me a few, so I could practise either getting out the way or playing off the back foot. After the net I would walk out to the middle with my bat and gloves and stand at each end for five minutes visualizing the different types of deliveries I would be facing.'

All the textbooks say that each ball should be played on its merits, and that shots should not be pre-determined, but most batsmen don't play in this way. Part of the preparation is to decide in advance what shots he will use against different bowlers. Clearly if a batsman decides to limit his shot selection to just the drive then he will be in trouble against the short ball, but if used with discernment pre-selection can be productive. Against fast bowling a batsman does not have time to decide that he will hook if he waits to make the decision until the ball has left the bowler's hand. He must have decided for himself before he begins his innings whether to hook if the ball is short. Pre-selection also applies to spin bowling, as Mike Brearley points out. 'On a turning wicket you set yourself to sweep, and you sweep on length. Alan Knott and Denis Compton would do this. They would sweep a good length ball regardless of whether it pitched outside the off stump or the leg stump, and if the ball was other than on a length they would improvise.'

Most batsmen eventually work out a method that works for them, and they can get very irritated if their preparation is disrupted. Brian Mason recalls sending a message to David Gower in the England dressing-room at Headingley in 1992 several hours before he was due to bat, and was taken aback to see how irritated

Gower was to be disturbed. 'When he realized that I only wanted to ask him a simple question he calmed down a bit, but I hadn't been aware until then how long he spent cocooning himself to get himself psyched up.'

Perhaps the most important part of any preparation is to recognize that things can go wrong, as David Gower is well aware. 'You try to stick to a routine, and you hope that by the time you pick up your bat to walk to the middle that the right responses will come naturally. But it doesn't always work. While you are waiting to bat all sorts of things will cross your mind, some of them good and some not so good. If you rely on a rigid routine to get you through you will be suicidal on the bad days; you have to adapt to every influence be it on or off the cricket field and come up with a way of coping with all circumstances, the highs and the lows. The highs are dangerous in their own way, because you often forget to think about what you are doing and why you are doing it when you're on a high. When that happens things start to go wrong.'

ROBIN'S STORY

Cricket is a technical game. There are people who will do exceptionally well for five or six seasons without much technical skill, but to stay at the highest level for a long time you do need a good technique. My good friend Allan Lamb hasn't got the best of techniques; the reason he's played for such a long time is because he has a fantastic eye for the ball. His lack of technique shows in his record. He will undoubtedly say that records don't bother him, but a Test average in the middle 30s is poor for a player of his quality. By contrast his overall first-class average compares with any of the best batsmen, but the bowling in county cricket isn't as demanding as at Test level.

If you don't have a solid technique you have nothing to fall back on when things go badly, so I've always made a point of working hard at that side of my game. I remember arriving at the ground for a game in 1984 to find Clive Lloyd was already out on the field getting himself ready. I told him that I couldn't believe how hard he was working, and he replied that when he was my age he didn't need to practise a great deal, but the older he became his eyesight got worse his reflexes got slower and he needed to work harder at his game now than at any other time of his career. This is probably what Graham Gooch is finding at the moment. Goochie's example has been a tremendous inspiration to me, because I can see that if I'm willing to continue to work hard I too can prolong my career till I'm 40.

The time that I spend in the nets is designed to improve my technical skills, but it is also what makes me feel mentally prepared to play Test cricket. I've always felt that I'm basically quite lazy, so I've felt the need to push myself to compensate. I don't take it to extremes; if someone says: 'Come on Judge, what about a few more throw downs', I'll say no if I think I've worked hard enough, but often I'll think that I could benefit from that little extra bit of practice. I also like to socialize in the evenings, and training is my way of making up for those evenings when I've eaten and drunk too well.

I practise hard because it suits me, and not because it's what others might expect. What works for me, won't work for everyone, and I believe that team managements should be sensitive to what different players need. You can't treat David Gower in the same way as Phil Tufnell, nor Devon Malcolm in the same way as me. I think that David should have been allowed to have the odd day off to do whatever he wanted, providing he was delivering the goods in the Test matches; and his Test record was excellent on that tour. The time to point the finger is when someone is not performing in the middle. I don't give a damn how much practice anyone else does; all I care about is that I'm happy with my game. It doesn't bother me that someone might have their feet up in the dressing-room. If a bowler has had a long spell the day before, let him have a lie in. I'm not going to be moaning that others are sitting round the swimming-pool, because I know what I need to do to fulfil my personal ambitions, and I'll make sure that I do it.

From time to time you can't prepare as you would like, as David found out on that Australian tour. If your philosophy is different to the skipper and the manager's then you just have to bite the bullet, because what they say must go. My physical preparation conforms fairly closely to Graham Gooch and Micky Stewart's ideas on the subject, but even I have had my difficulties. On that same Australian tour, on the morning of the last Test at the WACA, I woke up feeling positive, and went off for a net session with my brother at 8.30. For the first time on that tour I began to play with confidence; my drives were impeccable, my cuts were superb, and I thought to myself: 'Here we go, this is the game.' At about 9.30, Micky Stewart came over and said that it was time to warm up with the rest of the team. It was an extremely hot morning, my shirt was already saturated with sweat, and the last thing I needed was to warm up. I explained to Micky that I was finally feeling in the groove and that what I needed was to continue my net. He insisted that I join the rest of the side for the warm up, and by the time it was over I had actually cooled down, and the inspiration to continue my net had deserted me.

Perhaps the only time in my life that I haven't practised as hard as I could was last year, and this could explain why I didn't do as well in the middle of the season as I should have. But there again I wasn't practising any harder towards the end of the season when I was playing as well as at any time in my life. Maybe this shows that it's not just the amount of practice you put in that counts, but also the state of mind with which you approach it. A short practice approached positively may be of more benefit than a long half-hearted one. Net practice can have its limitations; the presence of the net can make the batsman feel claustrophobic, and bowlers often don't bowl properly. I don't know why because it's no practice for them, but they often overstep the crease by half a yard, and so not only do you have less time to pick up the flight of the ball, but you are playing a trajectory that you can never face in the middle.

My practice is designed to make me feel comfortable at the crease. Nick Faldo can hit a 1000 practice shots and on each occasion his swing will be an exact replica of the one he will use in a tournament; I can get someone to bowl me a 1000 balls to square cut in the nets, and not one of them will be exactly the same as a ball I get in the middle. So the idea is to reach a level of familiarity where I can face any situation in the middle with confidence. It's no fun practising the things you don't want to, but this is precisely what you need to do. It's tough facing short-pitched bowling; you've got to be fairly masochistic to ask bowlers to run in off 18 yards and bowl quickly at your head, but I've always made a point of doing it. Graeme Hick has often been in trouble against the short ball in recent years, and yet when we've been in adjacent nets I've been bobbing and weaving and he's been hitting cover drives. Practising the cover drive is all very well, but if you are weak against short-pitched bowling you're never going to be around long enough to use it. Facing fast bouncers makes extreme psychological demands on a batsman, and the only way to come to terms with it is to practise. You can set the bowling machine to half pace to start with so that you can get used to getting out the way, and as your confidence increases you can turn up the speed of the machine. Fast bowling is less frightening if you don't think you are going to get hit on the head. I've only been hit on the helmet twice in my career; in Antigua when I was mentally and physically exhausted, and at the Oval last year when I was too early on a pull. Hicky once scored 170 for Worcester against us but was hit on the helmet twice in the same innings. It didn't seem to bother him too much, but getting hit can't do anyone's confidence any good. Graeme is a tremendous player whose first-class record is far better than mine, but I'm sure if he could become more confident against the short ball he would be even better, and one way to gain that confidence is to practise.

It's very important to me that I should feel relaxed at the wicket, and that the bat should feel right in my hands. I'm not a graceful player in the mould of David Gower, and I like a heavy bat with much of the weight distributed towards the toe end of the blade, which suits my punchy style of play. Dean Jones paid me a compliment last year that meant a great deal: he said that the bat looked better in my hands compared to anyone else he had watched. I have quite an open stance, with my bat positioned in front of my back leg. This developed in Australia after I played too soon after a haemarrhoid operation and discomfort forced me to stand with my legs wide apart. I made some runs and felt surprisingly good. As I recovered I closed the stance up slightly, but basically it has remained the same since then. I know the right position for my hands to the last millimetre. This is vital because when I'm not feeling positive my mind has a funny way of telling me that my hands aren't in the right position even if they are. Now I know that when this happens I need to feed myself messages to get me to believe that the bat is comfortable rather than move my hands.

People can get themselves into all sorts of odd positions if they allow their minds to rule unchecked. Over the years that I have played against Peter Willey his stance has become more and more open to the point where he was almost facing square leg. Kim Barnett is the same, only he stands outside the leg stump as well. I know that both of them move more into line as the bowler reaches his delivery stride, but one of the principles of batting is to keep your body and head as still as possible. I know their theory is that they are better equipped to deal with the ball moving in to them and that they can play with more freedom on the leg side, but they leave themselves terribly exposed to the ball that moves away. Everyone works on their stance but it should be kept within certain parameters. Cricket is a sideways on game, and the mind should not be persuaded otherwise.

No matter how much practice you put in you're not going to play well if you're not mentally ready for the challenge. I need to feel sharp. Curiously, I often prefer it if I haven't played too well in my morning net because it gets the adrenalin going, and gives me the edge I'm looking for. If I've played well I have to remind myself that it's not going to be that easy. Occasionally a game is a non-starter; last summer I really didn't want to play in Hampshire's tour match against the Pakistanis. I felt that I could do with a few days off. Understandably the county didn't oblige me; it was a big game for the spectators and the sponsors, some of whom had come to see me play. Even so, I couldn't summon up the energy to banish all the negative thoughts I had about playing, and my performance reflected that.

Before each game I will think about which bowlers I will be facing and how the pitch will play. Some shots are pre-determined, and you have to work out whether it's worth playing them. Going down the wicket to a spinner is one such shot; when the ball goes above a certain flight line you can give it the charge, but only if you have already decided that this is the way to play. I am happy to do this against most spinners, but against bowlers with a good loop, like Phil Tufnell and Mushtaq Ahmed, the danger of being deceived in the flight and running straight past the ball is too great, as I learnt to my cost last summer. You can take pre-determination to extremes. I was chatting to Mark Ramprakash at lunch on the Saturday before he went out to bat against the Pakistanis at Headingley, and he was saying that he was going to block Mushtaq's first two balls, and if the third was anywhere near the right length he was going to sweep. He did and he was given out LBW. He was devastated about it at the time, but afterwards we had a laugh at the absurdity of it, because you just can't plan an innings like that.

If the pitch is likely to be fast I will do a lot of skipping a few days before to keep my feet light so that I will be quick enough to get out of the way of bouncers. I will also plan to play the line of the ball more than usual. Ideally I will feel as though my weight is moving in the direction of the ball without my body actually moving, so that I will be able to delay committing myself to a shot till the last moment. On a slow pitch where the short ball poses little threat, I will be looking to get much further forward to cover any variable bounce and movement.

On the morning of a game I will go out to the middle about an hour before the start, and have a look at the wicket. I shouldn't do it but I skid my bat across the surface to see how much moisture there is. If the grass stays brown I know the wicket will be hard, but if there is a tinge of green I know that it's still a little damp. I then take a few deep breaths and try to absorb my surroundings. I tell myself that this is what I want; that I enjoy the pressure. I will visualize the bowler running in, but I will stack the odds in my favour. The ball will appear very big and it won't deviate too much. I will pick up the movement early and it won't bother me. I will feel my head remaining steady, my bat going back straight, my feet light and moving into the right position. I will hear the sound of the ball hitting the middle of the bat, and if I've imagined an attacking shot I will see it bisect the fielders, race across the outfield, and hear it crash into the advertising hoardings on the boundary. My visualization will vary depending on where I'm playing. At Lord's the ball tends to run down the slope, so standing at the Nursery End I will see myself playing a great deal more at the ball, whereas at the Pavilion End I will be leaving more balls outside the off stump.

About forty minutes before the start of play, I go back to the dressing-room to put my feet up, have a cup of coffee, and read the paper. It's a time when I can relax and think about the day ahead. Batting at number four, I will have my thigh pad on from the start of the innings, and although I will have my bat, pads, gloves, and helmet laid out neatly, I don't pad up till the first wicket has fallen. To be honest, if the second wicket fell almost immediately, I would never be ready. It's never happened yet but I expect there will come a time. I wouldn't get timed out, because I would walk out carrying my pads if necessary, but I don't believe it would make any difference to how I played early on, because although I would be unprepared in a physical sense I would be mentally ready to play.

I tend to get quite nervous before I go out to bat. My palms become sweaty, and I find it difficult to sit quietly. I'll stretch, and do some squats. I'll read the various mental reminders like 'Stand Tall' and 'No Barrier is too Great' that I've written on the inside of my cricket coffin. I become very talkative, even more so than usual, and I actively participate in any dressing-room banter. I find that the repartee gets me thinking on my feet, sharpens up my mental reflexes, and helps to take my mind off my anxiety. I prefer not to watch the game too closely either from the balcony or on the TV. Batting can often seem to be a more terrifying proposition from the boundary. If someone is playing and missing a great deal it's easy to think that the bowler is bowling wonderfully well, when it's the batsman who is playing badly.

Other players have different routines and don't appear to be so outwardly nervous. Martin Crowe, and Viv Richards like to sleep before an innings; Viv will wake up when a wicket falls, splash his face with water, pop a stick of chewing gum in his mouth, and swagger out on to the pitch as if he hasn't a care in the world. Graeme Hick will sit still in front of the TV with his inners on, David Gower will be doing the crossword, while Allan Lamb will be sending off faxes and getting someone to put money on the horses. In reality I don't think that any of these players are much less nervous than me; it's just that they have other ways of coping with the stress.

Ideally, my preparation would be the same for every game, but things seldom work out that way. Sometimes my net sessions will go better than others; sometimes I will feel more relaxed than usual; sometimes it's a struggle to visualize properly, and at others I can live the experience in advance totally. Sometimes a change of circumstance in the dressing-room can upset me. In the Test match at Leeds last summer there was some question over whether I was going to bat at 3 or 4 because of Alec Stewart's wicket-keeping. If he had time for a long rest then I was to bat at 4, and if not at 3. When Goochie and Michael Atherton were still in at tea on the second day I felt sure I would be batting at 4, so I was very surprised to find that Alec still wanted me to bat at 3. In the event

I coped with the last hour's play and survived to make 24 not out.

Flexibility is the key to preparation; if everything had been geared towards me batting at 4 at Headingley, then I doubt if I would have lasted more than a few overs, because I would have been psychologically unprepared to bat. Being in the right frame of mind is vital, but part of that is recognizing that things may not always go to plan. An Olympic athlete knows months in advance exactly what time on what day he will be called upon to perform, and he has a fairly good idea of what will be required of him to do his best. Cricketers don't have that luxury; their preparation must be every bit as rigorous, but must have that extra ingredient of adaptability. Those that recognize this are the ones that are consistently successful and go on to have long and satisfying careers.

CHAPTER FOUR

MOTIVATION

Everyone sets goals for themselves; they may not be immediately apparent, and one might not be consciously aware of having set them, but they will be there, and if one probes the subconscious for long enough one will find them. Some goals are obvious; if someone has set their heart on owning a particular object he may work overtime to earn the money to get it, and a person will usually look before he crosses the road because he has a desire to live. Some people act in less rational ways, but are no less driven because of it. An alcoholic will be compelled to have a drink because he cannot tolerate the way he feels without it. Therefore the problem for a cricketer is not whether he is motivated or not, but whether he is motivated enough or in the right way. All elite sportsmen tend to be highly motivated, but what may differentiate the star performers from the pack is knowing what specific goals to set and how to fine tune them in order to achieve their best results.

Most cricketers don't have to think about why they are playing or what they want from the game as youngsters. Cricket will be just one of many sports, and those that go on to play seriously will be those who enjoyed it enough to be bothered. At this stage enjoyment will be sufficient motivation, and more often than not there will be a direct correlation between how much they enjoy the game and how good they are at it. The enjoyment will still be enough at the beginning of a professional career. Everything the young cricketer does will be new and present fresh challenges, so by and large he will be content just to be part of the county set-up.

As time goes by he needs to work out what is required of him to keep him in a job and to get satisfaction from it; to do so he has to think of motivation in a deeper sense, as David Gower explains: 'The sheer fact that you're repeating the same actions over a period of time means that you lose your naivety. You then have to look inside yourself to see what really motivates you and to set the appropriate goals. Every day you have to recogniZe what your challenge for that day will be and make it your goal or you won't succeed.'

While it is probably fair to say that the long-term goal of most county cricketers would be either to play for their country or continue to do so, players may set themselves all sorts of short term goals to achieve this target. This is where the cricketer needs a sense of self-awareness to know what will make him respond best. Chris Smith was partly driven by the knowledge that he was not as good a cricketer as Robin. 'I wanted to prove that I, with my average talent, could score more runs in day to day county cricket through the application of good, solid, positive principles than Robin could with his prodigious talent. I used to bait Robin and the rest of the team. At the beginning of the season I would call myself the hare and I would tell the boys that they would be chasing the hare that season, because the hare would be scoring 1800 runs. I don't know the exact figures but I reckon I was Hampshire's leading run scorer in 8 or 9 of the 12 years that I was there. It was a friendly, healthy rivalry; it kept me honest and Robin on his toes, because he knew it was important to me to score a lot of runs.'

Geoff Boycott is an object lesson in self-motivation. His aching hunger to score runs at any cost meant that he adopted a very single-minded approach. He gave the impression that, even if he was playing in a charity match against some schoolboys, he would give no quarter because losing his wicket would render him inconsolable, and retiring was unthinkable. No game was too inconsequential, no situation too meaningless, for Boycott to be focused on anything other than staying at the wicket and accumulating runs.

Scoring runs was never sufficient motivation for David Gower. 'I need to feel that there's some purpose to what I'm doing beyond just notching up runs. Ideally the team will have a set target and the challenge will present itself. If I go out to bat at 50-3 there's an obvious demand on me, but if I go out at 500-3 it's harder to feel that sense of purpose; the team has plenty of runs and in all probability we'll be declaring soon. Under those circumstances I have to find other ways of motivating myself. One way is the individual confrontation. Whenever I come up against a bowler that I particularly admire and rate highly there is the challenge of playing well against him. I loved playing against Dennis Lillee, and the gladiatorial nature of the combat appealed to me. When there are men like him to play against there is both one's reputation at stake and the fear that if you don't motivate yourself you will get hit, and so you take it seriously. There are times when motivation comes all by itself. I find that the spur of playing for England with the inbuilt atmosphere of a large crowd is enough to get me going, and the motivation comes from just being there. The challenge is laid on; you're playing amongst the best at the highest level, and if you succeed your reputation is secure. It's difficult to go back to county cricket after a Test; it's like going from one end of the spectrum to the other. Playing in an empty county ground can seem less important, but if you allow this feeling to take over and you forget to re-motivate yourself then the game will beat you.'

There can't be too much wrong with either Boycott or Gower's motivation as they are England's two leading run scorers, but both approaches do have their drawbacks. Boycott was fond of saying that what was good for him was good for the team; frequently this was true, and on these occasions there was nothing wrong with his single-mindedness. Yet there are times when the needs of the team will be different; then it helps to have players who are equally motivated by team success as by individual success. If someone scores 150 in eight hours when what was required was 100 in three hours then the team has a problem. In this case the batsman who is prepared to risk sacrificing his wicket in the interests of the team is of more value. When one compares David Gower's first-class county record with his Test record it is clear that he hasn't always been able to find the motivation to lift his game when the challenge does not inspire him.

Ideally one should be able to motivate oneself in a way that encompasses both the needs of the individual and the team, because not only will one's own game be improved, but there is also no danger that one's approach will serve to de-motivate other members of one's team. However any attempts to impose such motivation are almost certainly doomed to failure if they are not sympathetic to that person's character. So to some extent all any team manager can do is to pick players that are motivated in that way, or to accept that some may not be, but are worth having in the team anyway because they have exceptional cricketing ability.

Grayson Heath identifies the desire to be a match winner in any situation as the ideal motivation. 'Every year in Natal there is a cricket week in which boys from all the schools play against each other to see who will go on to play for the province's schools' XI. In his last year at school Chris asked me what he needed to do during this week to be selected for the Natal schools' side. I was rather taken aback because I had never been asked a question like this, but I thought feverishly for a while, and I came up with an answer that I'm still proud of, since it holds good at all levels of cricket. Chris had five games, beginning on the Monday and ending on the Friday, and to my mind there were two ways of approaching it. He could set out on the Monday simply striving to play his way into the Natal side. This way he would be totally selfish, and would either succeed or fail in his endeavours that Monday. If he succeeded there were still four days to go and so there would still be an element of uncertainty. If he failed he would be utterly miserable because he had wasted one day. And so it would continue throughout the week. The other approach would be to walk out on the Monday and try to win the game for his team. If he succeeded he would at least be guaranteed ten smiling faces and the pleasure that comes with knowing you've won the game for your team. Since he would have derived pleasure from that first game, he would be in a better frame of mind for the following days. If he failed he would be no worse off than if he had adopted the attitude of playing for himself. It's important for a person to realize that their own personal contribution to the team effort is critical at all times, but also to remember that it is a team game and that success is not measured by one's ability to acquire runs but by one's ability to win games.'

Setting goals focuses a person's attention on what he wants and how to get it. These goals will be divided into short-term and long- term goals, but both need constant monitoring. A batsman's first goal when he goes out to bat may well be to get off the mark; if he doesn't switch to another goal once this is achieved he may struggle. Greg Chappell used to count off the runs in 10s. Once he had made 10 his next goal would be 20 and so on. Likewise long-term goals need to be revised, if not as frequently. Dr Graham Jones points out that it had been an ambition of Lisa Opie's to win the British Open Squash championship ever since she was at school; once she had eventually achieved it she needed a new target. Brian Mason remembers talking to David Gower after he had been recalled to the England side during the summer of 1992 and asking him what his new goal was. Gower's reply of doing enough to keep his place in the side worried Brian Mason. 'You need tangible goals; it's not enough to set yourself a target of maintaining your place. If you aim to stay still you will go backwards. You see it in football the whole time. A club can strive hard to get promoted to the Premier division and succeed, but if it fails to set itself a new target beyond staying up it will probably go straight back down again. What David needed to do was to set himself some specific personal targets like 10,000 Test runs or a certain number of Test matches.'

All goals must be realistic. There is no point setting a goal that is beyond the reach of a performer. A player who has a long-term goal of scoring 5,000 Test runs when he will be lucky to play in more than a handful of Test matches will in time become demoralized and demotivated. Dominic Cork's bowling performance in his first one-day international at Old Trafford last summer suggests that his goal setting was well-judged, even if it was not consciously determined. If he had gone into the game with the attitude that wickets were all important, he might have become dispirited when Aamir Sohail was dropped off his fourth ball. Instead, he maintained his composure and turned in a tidy spell. He recognized that he had no control over whether the batsman hit the ball or the fielder caught it, and centred his efforts on putting the ball in the right place to limit the batsman's attacking options.

Goals can be outcome or process oriented. Typical outcome goals for a batsman would be to set a target of a certain number of runs for the season, winning an England cap, or helping his county to win a trophy. A process goal would be to set out to play as best as he possibly could, or in a certain kind of way. Occasionally the two can overlap; when Graham Gooch prepared to take on the Indians in the semi-final of the World Cup in 1987 he set himself the process goal of sweeping the spinners, and in doing this successfully he achieved the outcome goal of winning the match.

Outcome goals provide a greater motivation, but theory proposes that process goals are better suited to sportsmen because that is what they have control over. An athlete has no power over whether someone else runs faster than he does; a batsman has no power over whether the bowler produces the unplayable delivery. All he can do is his best, and if that is all he sets out to do and he achieves it regardless of the outcome, then his confidence won't suffer. Perversely, experience shows that many sportsmen turn theory on its head and opt for outcome goals. Chris Smith is one such cricketer. 'When there were 24 county championship games I would break the season up into three segments of eight games each, and my target would be 600 runs for each segment. These targets weren't just idle fantasy; I would write them down and pin them on the back of various doors in the house, on the inside of my cricket case, and I would read them every day. I would fill in my scores after every game and I would know exactly how many runs I needed in the rest of the fixtures to reach the target. Scoring these runs was very important to me, and if I was in the middle of a bad trot I was never as perky as when things were going well. Having these targets meant I was determined to get the most out of every opportunity, and that I learned the art of batting 'time'. This is a weakness of Robin's; he scores too many pretty 100s and quick 50s and doesn't go on to turn them into big hundreds and double hundreds. To do this you have to be prepared to bat for a full day. When he masters this he will be unstoppable.'

Goals are the building bricks of confidence. As each goal is achieved the cricketer's faith in his ability increases, and the belief that he can meet future targets grows. Those that know what drives them and can harness it by setting their goals wisely have an incalculable advantage. Motivation is no substitute for talent, but it will ensure that someone puts in the necessary hard work to make the best of his ability.

ROBIN'S STORY

My ultimate goal is to be involved in a happy family, and I believe that the most meaningful measure of my success is my capacity to be a good father and a loving husband. My cricket career will finish when I'm about 40, but my family will be with me for the rest of my life. Obviously, success on the cricket field is important to me. Quite apart from the personal satisfaction I get from my achievements, the material rewards that I have received from the game have been immense, and have enabled me to provide the standard of living for Kathy and Harrison that I would want them to have. In the pre-Packer era playing Test cricket brought prestige and recognition; it now brings money as well. A top Test player can earn over £100,000 per year which is a good living, and a great incentive to play Test cricket. Test cricketers attract sponsors, and, although my endorsement contracts are not performance related, I can be fairly certain that my contracts won't be renewed if my performances tail off and I find myself out of the Test team for any length of time. If this happens I can expect my income to be cut by three-quarters.

Having said that, I would still want to play cricket professionally even if I wasn't good enough to play at Test level, so the money is by no means my most important motivation. I love the game, I enjoy the cricketing way of life, and I've made a lot of friends playing it. Sometimes it's easy to get fed up with the game, especially if you're fielding on the boundary on a cold afternoon in a match that's going nowhere in front of a handful of snoring spectators. When I catch myself thinking like that I remind myself that there are far worse ways of being paid to spend one's time than running around outdoors chasing a bit of red leather. I've never found the prospect of office life that attractive and when it came to choosing between going into my father's business or playing professional cricket there wasn't too much competition. Since then I've never thought about doing anything other than playing cricket. The furthest I've got in contemplating a career after I retire is to spend two years getting my golf in shape and then joining the senior pro tour!

My highly competitive nature combined with having my father's philosophy of 'If you do something, you do it properly' drummed into me from an early age means that I have a strong internal drive to succeed, and that the lazy side of my character often gets overruled. I like to do well at anything I attempt. At home, I can't go for a run just for the sake of it. I have to push myself; I go on the same circuit each time I go out, make a note of how long I've taken, and get disappointed if I haven't improved. I know it's the complete opposite of the way you are supposed to approach running, but I can't do it any other way. If I don't come back feeling shattered, I don't feel as if I have done myself justice.

I take a tremendous pride in the things I do and I don't like to have that pride dented. I'm a sensitive person; I know that I take some criticism far more seriously than is intended, but even so I find it hurtful. It would probably be better for my peace of mind if I could shrug it off by acknowledging to myself that sometimes you play well and others you don't, and that what anybody else says doesn't matter that much, providing you learn from the experience. However, it's not like that at the moment, and I find the prospect of being humiliated in the tabloids by being portrayed with a dunce's cap on my head is a great motivational spur.

When I first started to play cricket professionally I never set myself particular goals. I may have had some vague idea of scoring 800 runs in a season for the Hampshire seconds, but basically it was just exciting to be there, and my main aim was simply to do well in the next game. I had no expectations of playing regularly for the first team when I arrived because I was just one of four overseas players. Gordon Greenidge, Malcolm Marshall, and my brother would clearly take precedence over me, and there was a four year qualification period before I could be registered as an English player. It felt slightly anti-climactic to return to Hampshire for my second season, because I had been playing first-class cricket for Natal during the winter and I knew that I was coming back to second team cricket. Nevertheless it was still something of a novelty, and the prospect of the World Cup the following season, when Malcolm and Gordon would be away for six weeks with the West Indies, made me determined to score as heavily as possible, so that when my chance came I would be certain to be selected.

It was my brother who encouraged me to take goal setting seriously when I started playing for the first team. We would divide the season into three sections and set a target of 600 runs for each. The idea was that the prospect of scoring 1800 runs in the championship was a fairly daunting prospect when viewed as a single target, but when split up into manageable sections it became easier to imagine reaching it. Quite apart from the challenge of aiming for a set number of runs, having my brother saying: 'I'm telling you here and now that I will be scoring more runs than you' was more than enough to gee me up in itself. I've always believed in setting goals that are on the high side, though always within the bounds of reality, because if you only just fail to meet a high target you will have still done very well.

I was having a chat with Tony Middleton before the start of last season about his run target for the summer. I've always been fond of Tony, and I was sorry that there hadn't been many first team opportunities for him at Hampshire while my brother was at the club. Now that Kippy had retired Tony was certain to play the full season and I was interested to see how he approached it. At first he was reluctant to tell me, and it was only when I reminded him that I was his friend and was trying to help him, that he confided in me that he thought 1200 runs in his first full season would be a good effort. I told him that I thought that would be a poor standard. As an opener he could expect to have 40 innings and only to average 30 would be selling himself short. He was going to be playing on a number of flat wickets against weakened bowling attacks, and he should be setting his sights much higher. If he set a target of 1200 and fell just short he was going to end the season with a 1000 runs, but if he set a much higher target and fell just short he would have achieved something of which to be proud. You've got to strive for perfection and be satisfied with a bit less. I'm not sure whether he did revise his target upwards, but he certainly proved that 1200 runs was ridiculously low for him because he finished the season with nearly 1800 runs, and was deservedly picked for the England A tour as a result.

Since I began playing for England I've had to rethink my targets for Hampshire. Now I can no longer predict how many county championship games I will be playing, and to set a target of 1500 runs would be absurd. I was unhappy with my total of 700 runs last season; I didn't consciously set myself a run target, but I suppose that I would have been happy with 1000-1200 runs. Instead, I made my goal to play a major role in Hampshire winning a one-day trophy. The year before last I was voted Man of the Match in the Nat West final, and I also collected a couple of awards earlier in the competition, so I felt that I had contributed fairly strongly to Hampshire's victory. I was pleased with that, and so I decided to make that my target again for last season, and I was delighted to pick up a couple of Man of the Match awards in the early rounds of the Benson & Hedges, and again in the final. In retrospect, I may have undersold myself because I had achieved my objective halfway through the season, so in future my goal might be to contribute to Hampshire winning more than one competition in a season. Nevertheless, I don't think my one-day form fell apart, because I batted well opening the innings in the Sunday League and the club managed to finish third in the table. We needed to win our last game against Leicester to be sure of third spot, so I was pumped up for that game, though as it turned out it rained all across the country and we clinched our place without playing.

My Hampshire colleagues are a great source of inspiration to me. I like to think I'm quite popular in the dressing-room, and I've made some wonderful friends at the club, so I want to do well as much for them as for myself. I would hate for them to think that I'm happy to collect my England bonuses and that when I play with them it's a bit of a joke. I've played with some prima donnas in my time, and I've always disliked that attitude. They're entitled to let themselves down, but not their team mates. County players have their own pride and their own bonuses to aim for. £1000 pounds for coming third in the Sunday League might not be so financially motivating for me, but for some players it is desperately important and I try never to forget that. I'm also conscious that the club have always been generous to me, and I'm well paid by them for what I do. I've heard that Wasim and Waqar are on incredible salaries at Lancashire and Surrey, and good luck to them. As a batter I don't have the same bargaining power, and besides I've never needed to ask the club for any more. I only play about half the season for them, and I want to give back something for what they have given me in the past.

There are times when it is difficult to get motivated playing in county cricket. I think it happens to everyone who plays at Test level. You come back to the county and you're mentally and physically exhausted after five days in which you've done nothing but eat, drink, talk, sleep, and play cricket. There is no escape even at the hotel; people approach you while you're trying to switch off, expecting you to discuss the day's play with them. So when you return to the county it's hard to find that hunger. If the side is 250-2 and you've already made 100, it's not that easy to summon up the desire to press on and convert the hundred into a double hundred. I tend to think that there's a lot of other batsmen in the team who can get some runs, so why not let them? It's somewhat different if you are chasing a specific target because then there is a challenge that is important to the side. If you get out to a poor shot when you've made a century and the team still needs plenty of runs, you go back to the dressing-room and just one glance at your team mates' faces tells you that you've let them down.

I know that this isn't quite the right attitude, and that I ought to want to score runs for the county in any circumstances, but to be honest I'm not particularly interested in changing it. My biggest motivation is to win games for Hampshire. With the greatest of respect to Jimmy Cook, he used to regularly grind out big hundreds for Somerset, but he spent so long doing it that where did it get them? It was great for Jimmy, and sometimes for the county, but there are times when you have to press on and accelerate. Scoring runs doesn't make me nearly as happy as the sound of champagne corks popping and a row of smiling faces in the dressing-room.

The only time that I have been concerned about my attitude was towards the end of last season. It was after the Texaco games against Pakistan, where I had picked up a couple of Man of the Match awards as well as the Man of the Series. I was on a bit of a high, there had been a number of late nights what with the end of series parties, including Micky Stewart's leaving party, and I felt completely flat for Hampshire's game against Durham at Darlington. For the first time in my life I wasn't jumping around before I went to bat; instead I curled up in a corner and went to sleep. I was out for 1 and I don't even know how I got that. In the second innings I was determined to battle it out, but my mind just wouldn't let me. Half of me wanted to do it for everyone else, and the other half was saying: 'Forget it I'm knackered, I don't want to do anything'. Inevitably I was out for 3. I was so worried about this mental state that I talked to the club about it. They were extremely understanding; they were pleased that I had recognized that my motivation was low and I was capable of talking to them about it, and thought that to acknowledge what was happening to me was halfway to solving the problem.

Things improved slightly for the next game against Essex. Although Hampshire weren't in contention for the championship, I was keen to do well because no one wants to hand Essex the title on a plate, and there was also the small matter of impressing Graham Gooch and Keith Fletcher. I felt good for about an hour and a half and then all of a sudden I lost it, because my heart just wasn't in it. I had a chat with Keith Fletcher about it afterwards. I asked him how Goochie maintained his hunger to score big runs innings after innings, season after season. He replied that Gooch had had his problems in the seventies, but in the last ten years Essex had won the championship five times, and never been out of the top four, so he had always had something to play for. That's why he's always seemed a little greedier than everyone else. It hasn't been that way at Hampshire, but even so I ought to be able to do a little better.

I'm extremely wary of declaring my goals in public. At the beginning of the season reporters ask me what my goals are for the season, but I'm only prepared to make general statements rather than commit myself to precise figures. I'll say things like: 'I want to help the club win the championship' because that's only partially down to me, and 'I want to keep my place in the England side' because it would be silly to say anything else. I don't want to say I'm going to score a certain amount of runs and risk making a complete berk of myself in public if I fail to get them. I can remember Barry Richards coming over to this country and saying he was going to score 2000 runs in the season. He made 0 in his first innings and immediately some wise guy came up to him and said: 'You've got a long way to go.' I suppose if I was more confident I would be making these kinds of statements, but I'm not. I also think it's incredibly arrogant to say this sort of thing, and I dislike arrogance. I know what my targets are, I know if I've failed to meet them, I know if I've let myself and the team down, so why bother to go public about it?

No one should have to motivate themselves to play Test cricket. The fact that you are playing against the best in front of thousands of spectators at the ground and millions more watching at home on TV gets the adrenalin pumping round the system. The problem at Test level is not whether you can take the game seriously but whether you can handle the pressure of the occasion. I enjoy the big match atmosphere, and I like the feeling of being under pressure. There is something very exciting about pitting your skills against the world's best, and I've had my fair share of head to heads with opposition bowlers. It's a great challenge to try to dominate bowlers like Ambrose, Bishop, Hughes, Reid, Wasim, Waqar, and Mushtaq, and at times the confrontations become verbal. On the Australian tour to England in 1989 I had a number of conversations with Merv Hughes whilst I was batting. Once after I had played and missed he shouted: 'You can't effing bat to save your life.' The next ball I smacked him for four and as I ran past him I said: 'Make a good pair, don't we. I can't effing bat, and you can't effing bowl.' Waqar was equally chatty last summer, but I have to watch myself now that the TV coverage is from behind the bowler's arm at each end, because the bowler can say anything he likes and no one is any the wiser, but everyone can see me having a go at him. Confrontations like these certainly give the game an edge; I hate getting out at the best of times, but giving someone like Waqar the pleasure of dismissing me is too much. Waqar only got me out once during the series, in the second innings at Headingley, but that dismissal gave me more pain than any other.

After I had played a few Test matches and grew in confidence that my career would span more than a handful of matches, I began to set myself a few targets for Test cricket. My long-term goal is to score 7000 runs by the time I have played 100 Tests. I realize that is aiming high because I've only played 40 Tests and a lot depends on my form and fitness, but I think that if you reach that figure you are marked down as a great player. I was playing on both occaions when David Gower and Gordon Greenidge reached their 7000 runs in their 100th Test and if I can reach the same standard as them I will be happy. Of course it would be nice to get ahead of the target by reaching 4000 runs in my 50th Test, and I have made that mark a medium-term goal.

As far as each game is concerned I set myself a target of a certain number of runs. Kath always asks me what I'll be satisfied with before I leave. Usually I will say that if I score under 50 in the match I will be bloody disappointed, if I make 65–75 I will be satisfied, and I'll be delighted with anything over 80. But these are only guidelines; obviously if the pitch is very poor I would be satisfied with less, and equally if I only scored an aggregate of 70 in every game I would be disappointed because a career average of 35 would be distinctly ordinary. By the same token, if I made 0 in the first innings I would welcome 50 in the second with open arms.

I am aware that I've generally scored better in the first innings than in the second, and it has crossed my mind that perhaps sometimes I relax too much in the second innings knowing that I've already got my target for the match. However, I feel that this is a coincidence more than anything else. Often in the second innings you will be after some quick runs to set a declaration, or you will be left not out at the end of the game, or the pitch will be noticeably more worn. I'm not aware of relaxing, because when I'm out in the middle there are plenty of innings to make up for when I haven't got my quota of runs.

Throughout an innings I have three run targets; 50, 70 which is my match goal, and 100. It's nice to score 50s and 100s but they don't have the same significance for me as they do for some players. A score of 45 or 95 is still a good effort. In fact I mind missing out on a 50 much more than a hundred, because if you're within sight of a hundred you've got plenty of runs in the bag anyway. Getting off the mark is no big deal to me; I've had a lot of 0s and it doesn't bother me. People used to make such a big thing about David Gower's record sequence of innings without a 0 for England, which was finally ended in Melbourne in 1990. I can't see what's so important about one run, and besides, left handers often find it relatively simple to get off the mark because bowlers tend to stray down the leg side early in their innings as they struggle to find their line.

The lunch and tea intervals also make good short-term goals, and whilst batting I keep myself going by saying to myself: 'Be there at the end of the session.' However, generally speaking, runs are what count. People won't look back at the record books in years to come and say: 'Ah yes, Robin Smith batted for over 100 minutes.' All they will see is that I was out for 17 and that I failed. Getting the team into a winning position is what matters to me, and for that one needs runs. Therefore my usual approach is to go for my strokes if the ball is there to be hit. I don't mind scoring 3 in 10 overs if I'm trying to attack, but if I'm prodding around trying to defend I lose confidence and give the bowlers the advantage. There are exceptions. Against the West Indies in Barbados in 1990 runs were immaterial. Then I was quite happy to bat for hours on end for 40 because it was what the team needed, as we had to bat throughout the last day to save the game.

Occasionally I will make it my goal to bat in a certain type of way. In the first innings of the Lord's Test against the Australians in 1989 I was out for 32 trying to pull Lawson. I was furious with myself, because I had been batting well. I had even had a bit of luck a few runs earlier when Steve Waugh had had a good shout for leg before turned down by Nigel Plews, and I had said to myself: 'I'm on to my second dig here, so let's cash in.' The Australians went on to score a huge total in their first innings, and we knew that we were going to have to bat for two days to save the game. We had already lost the first Test at Headingley and we felt that if we lost this one then the series was as good as over. I knew that the Australians were going to try to bounce me out, and

Old Trafford 1992. Man of the Match in the final One-day International against Pakistan.

Robin in South Africa, aged 10, practising the pull shot for Barry Richards' coaching manual . . . . .

. . . . . and using it to great effect for Hants.

C. Cole/Allsport

Playing for his school, aged 11.

Christopher in the nets at home in South Africa.

Poise, power and timing, aged 15.

Robin and Christopher at Southampton.

At home with Kathy and Harrison.

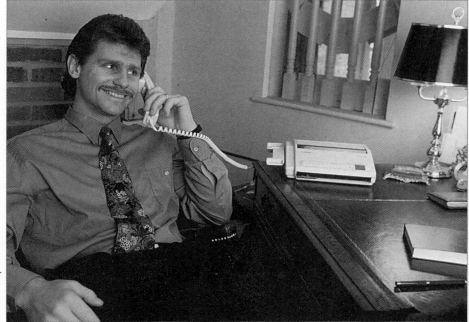

Home alone.

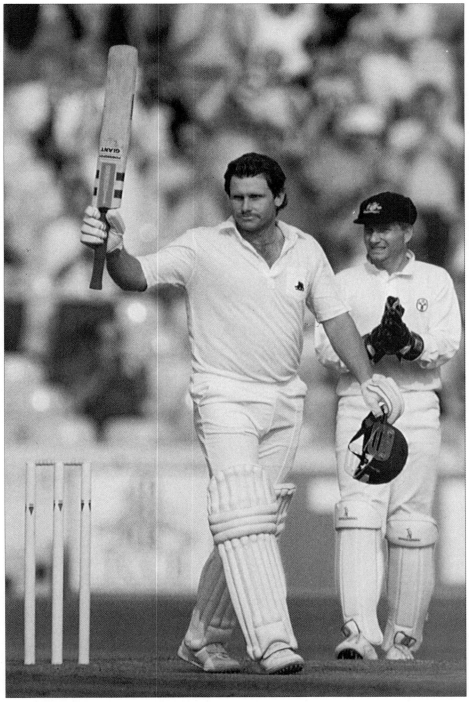

Old Trafford 1989. Acknowledging his first test century against Australia.

Lord's 1990. The softest dismissal – Hit wicket b. Bracewell 0.

There are worse ways to earn a living (Australia 1990).

The morning after the night before (Australia 1990).

The Oval 1991. Meeting fire with fire in the final test against the West Indies.

B. Radford/Allsport

Mushtaq eat your heart out.

A. Murrell/Allsport

Lord's 1992. Getting the better of Mushtaq in the first One-Day International against Pakistan.

The Oval 1992. Time out in his unbeaten innings of 84 against Pakistan.

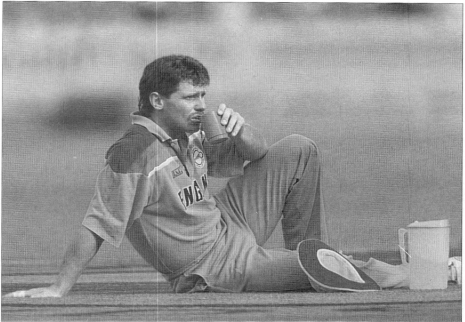

A. Murrell/Allsport

The World Cup tour to Australia that promised so much ended in disappointment for Robin and England.

D. Munden/Sportsline

Talking to the Old Master, India 1993.

The Lone Ranger in Bombay, 1993.

Getting it right in the nets, Bombay 1993.

Madras 1993. c Amre b Kumble for a defiant 56.

The trademark square cut.

so I was determined to cut out the pull. However my technique meant that I instinctively got in position to pull, and I had to consciously restrain myself from going through with the shot. The result was that Merv Hughes hit me time and again on the body. To the spectators and to certain members of the press it looked as if I was in terrible trouble, but I was quite happy playing like this. As long as I don't break any bones I don't mind a few bruises, and I've got a fair amount of natural padding anyway. My battering even came to the attention of the Queen because when the teams were presented to her after the tea interval she said to me: 'It doesn't look like you've got many friends out there.' Although we went on to lose that game, I was particularly proud of the way that I had played in the manner I had set out to, and I wasn't even that disconsolate at missing out on a maiden Test century by 4 runs.

I know it might seem a bit rich coming from someone who originally came to this country as an overseas player, but I do feel that overseas players are a mixed blessing in county cricket. Of course it's inspirational to play opposite people like Viv Richards, Courtney Walsh, Wasim, and Waqar, and their presence certainly raises the standard of first-class cricket in this country. However, I don't know if the advantages of improved county cricket are balanced out by their effect on English Test cricket. We can get used to playing against them, but more significantly they can get used to our players and conditions. I know that throughout his summer with Durham last season, Dean Jones was compiling a dossier on all the players and pitches, and he will have reported his findings to the rest of the Australian squad. A bowler like David Milns might have been an unknown quantity to the Australians, and it might have taken them a couple of Tests to work him out, but now they will know exactly what to expect, and England will have lost a slight edge.

Other countries act in their own interests, and I think we should too. I had three great years playing grade cricket in Western Australia, broke a 35-year-old record for the number of runs scored in a year, but I never came close to representing the state side even when there were Test matches or injuries. I remember there was one occasion when they were prepared to send a patently sub-standard state side on a 12 day tour of the Eastern states because they didn't want to give me any experience of batting on the wickets at the SCG or the Gabba which might have proved useful to me in a Test match later in my career. Malcolm Marshall is the first to admit that if it hadn't been for county cricket he would have been nowhere near as successful for the West Indies in this country. Allan Border spent a year with Essex during which he worked out Graham Gooch's weaknesses. It's not exactly demotivating to know that this is happening, but it is disheartening to feel that other countries have an advantage when playing us at home.

Some people have doubted my commitment and motivation to play for England because I wasn't born in this country. Of course South Africa has a special place in my heart, and I wish them well, but I no longer have any real ties with the country. Mum and Dad are planning to spend half the year in England and half in Perth; I have made my home here; I have an English wife; and I'm desperately proud of playing for my adopted country. I can't claim that I feel exactly the same way as someone who was born and grew up in England because I don't know what that feels like, but when I walk out to bat for England no one will be trying any harder. I feel an intense sense of loyalty to my England team mates, and even when South Africa were playing England at rugby last November I was cheering for the home side. I wasn't asked to join the rebel tour to South Africa in 1989, but even if I had been I wouldn't have gone. I've committed myself to playing for England, and will continue to do so for as long as possible.

A few players have found it demotivating that the ban on the South African tour rebels was lifted prematurely. I can understand Rob Bailey's disenchantment, because he turned down a lot of money to go and those who chose not to remain loyal to England were selected ahead of him for the tour to India. However, cricket's governing bodies have approved the lifting of the ban, and if that is the case then I am all for England choosing the best team from the players available. More than anything else I want to be part of a successful England side. Mike Gatting's return may put pressure on me for the number four batting spot, but that's all for the good of English cricket, and besides I believe that I have the ability to hold on to my position.

A captain can make all the difference to a team's motivation. That is not to say that players are not individually motivated to do well, but the captain can help to produce that extra edge that is sometimes the difference between a side's success and failure. I have always been motivated by captains who lead from the front and who command respect by the strength of their performance on the pitch. I have been very lucky in this respect to play for England under Graham Gooch, David Gower, and Allan Lamb. I think that Lamby's captaincy skills have been rather harshly judged, because whenever he captained the side it meant that our best batsman was not playing. A captain isn't a miracle worker; if he doesn't have the bowlers with the penetration to bowl sides out and if the batting continually collapses he won't win any games. However, there is more to captaincy than individual performance, and I found it difficult playing for Natal under Barry Richards because he didn't always seem to appreciate that everyone didn't have his level of genius and he couldn't understand why everyone didn't automatically do as they were told. A captain must know what motivates each member of his team, how to get the best out of each player, and if I have any criticism of Graham Gooch's captaincy it is that there is a tendency to treat all players in the same way.

Man management is a more valuable commodity in county cricket. At Test level players tend to have a greater sense of self-awareness, discipline, and motivation, but at county level there are many young players who have little sense of direction and need a strong guiding hand. Neither Nick Pocock or Mark Nicholas, my two captains at Hampshire, ever turned in what might be called regular match winning performances, and whilst that may have been frustrating at times for them and the other players, they have been a great asset to the club. Mark has always been helpful to me when I'm going through a bad patch, and he's very good at pointing out ways to improve one's game. One of his greatest pluses is that he likes to play attacking cricket, and I find that attitude highly motivating. He firmly believes that you don't win matches unless you give yourself a chance of losing them, and so Hampshire are rarely involved in dull draws. It's meant that we have lost more games than we otherwise might, but it's also given the younger players experience of playing under pressure, and that might have counted in our favour in our Nat West and Benson & Hedges victories in the last two seasons.

All players' motivational levels vary from time to time, and I am no exception, but if anyone needs a reminder of how important motivation is, he need look no further than David Gower. The difference between his attitude in 1991 and 1992 while playing for Hampshire was remarkable. It wasn't that he suddenly started running laps of the pitch or doing press-ups, or even that he was particularly pumped up at the crease last season, but that he had a more determined, focused look about him which showed through in his results. He had decided that he did have a cricketing future and was prepared to do what was necessary to get himself back into the England side.

Different people have different motivations and will need to set different goals to achieve what they want, but I feel that enjoyment has to be the foundation on which all goals are built. If you don't enjoy what you are doing it's so much harder to put the effort in to reach your targets. With that in mind, I think one of the top priorities for a cricketer is a sense of humour. Some of the grounds we play on have fairly basic facilities, and it can be tempting to think: 'What's it all about?' If you can have a good laugh about it, and still go out and do your best, you won't be going far wrong.

CHAPTER FIVE

CONCENTRATION

'Concentrate' shouts the coach as the batsman plays and misses outside the off stump. This is a scenario that is repeated time and again up and down the country, but if ever a batsman is given unhelpful advice then this is it. The batsman may be concentrating very hard, but on the wrong things; it is the focus of his attention that is crucial. Instead of concentrating on the bowler and the ball, he may be thinking about anything from what the slip fielders are talking about to what he is going to eat for dinner. He may even be aware that he is focusing on the wrong things, but be unsure what to do about it or even unable to do anything about it. Concentration is not some kind of activity, like paying bills, that one sometimes forgets to do, but a learned skill which can be worked on and improved.

How hard or how well someone is concentrating is no easy matter for an observer to judge. Geoff Boycott's single-minded approach to crease occupation and his capacity not to be distracted from it suggested a batsman with exceptional powers of concentration. Yet there are many sportsmen who perform extremely well even when they don't appear to be concentrating. John McEnroe always seemed to play his best tennis after being upset by a line call and having precipitated a row with the umpire; Derek Randall thrived on chatting to all those around him, and could even reduce such witty conversationalists as the Australian close fielders to asking him to shut up. Does David Gower's sometimes languid air at the crease betray a lack of concentration? If so, he has made an awful lot of runs at Test level by not paying attention.

Concentration is the art of being focused on an activity whilst at the same time being able to exclude irrelevant external information and the internal meanderings of one's mind. Without this focus, no performer will realize his true potential. Concentration is a skill that most people acquire as babies, forget as toddlers, and spend the rest of their lives trying to rediscover. A nine month old baby can be rapt in wonder at an apparently mundane object like a glass ball, and no amount of noise will distract him until he is ready to be so. The parents may neurotically worry that their baby has partial deafness, but the truth is that he is just concentrating on what he is doing. The problems come when the child becomes more aware of the outside world and more self-conscious about his role in it. As soon as he realizes there is an audience who will in some way be evaluating his performance, then keeping his attention tightly focused becomes more demanding, and the task itself becomes more difficult.

An adult can of course learn to control his powers of concentration. The baby spies the glass ball and becomes enthralled by it, rather than consciously seeking out the ball to make it the focus of his attention. An adult can decide when and where to focus. Sometimes the focus will need to be within a narrow band; an accountant will need to confine his attention to the figures on a page if he wants to do his calculations quickly and accurately. At other times one needs a much broader band of concentration; a driver needs to pay attention to the road ahead of him, the road behind him, suicidal pedestrians, and the weather conditions, if he is to negotiate getting from A to B with any degree of safety. Different sports make differing demands on the concentrational powers of the performers. A sprinter needs a narrow band of concentration, while a batsman needs to be able to switch between the narrow and the wide. Whilst the bowler is bowling he must restrict his attention to the ball, but if he fails to pay attention in between deliveries to the field settings, the weather, the condition of the pitch, and the state of the game, he is unlikely to last long. What is important is that the performer should recognize the demands of his sport, and focus his attention accordingly.

What makes Test cricket unique is the length of time over which it is played. There is no other game that takes 30 hours to play and takes place over 5 days; this makes exceptional demands on a batsman's concentration and raises the question of how long a person can keep his attention focused on one activity? School lessons usually last for 50 minutes, because the educational system is based on the psychological principle that this is the maximum length of time a teacher can expect to hold the attention of his class, though most teachers would probably argue that 50 seconds was a more realistic figure. No work has been done to discover if there is a limit to a sportsman's attention span. An athlete like Linford Christie has to channel his attention for an explosive burst of activity lasting under 10 seconds. For a batsman the requirements are completely different. Ideally he must be prepared to be at the crease for 4 or 5 hours, yet it is impossible to maintain absolute concentration for anything like this length of time without becoming psychologically exhausted. So a batsman must be able to switch from total concentration to relaxation, and back again, at will. Every batsman has his own methods of achieving this, though often it's a matter of commonsense. Greg Chappell used the bowler turning to start his run-up as the trigger to start attending, and switched off when the ball had gone dead. What matters is how well the batsman can do it.

Chris Smith believes there are no short cuts to learning how to concentrate like this for hours on end. 'The only way you can work at it is out in the middle. If you don't play cricket for 6 months over the winter it's almost impossible to bat all day in your first innings back, even if the bowling is indifferent. What I would do in that first game was to try and bat for a couple of hours. Once I'd done that, the idea of batting for 3 hours in the next game wasn't so intimidating, and so on. Gradually I would build up my powers of concentration so that I could bat all day. This is where the concept of batting 'time' is so important, because no amount of reading a book or net practice can teach you how to concentrate for a day.'

Another consequence of cricket's time factor is that what a batsman needs to concentrate on during the course of an innings may change. A high jumper's concentration will be focused on clearing the bar no matter how long the competition lasts. While the narrow band of the batsman's concentration will always be the ball, what he decides to do with it will be determined by his wider band of concentration - how he views his teams' needs. David Gower believes that this is often overlooked and that as a result there are a lot of myths about when a batsman is concentrating and when he isn't. 'Concentration is the art of knowing what is needed at any one time. It's too facile to say that if someone gets out, then he's lost concentration. He might not have lost concentration at all, but merely changed his outlook. People that say: 'He lost concentration' are working on the principle that one's only intention was to stay out there. For the compilers of runs, whose mantra is always the same - 'I will not get out', getting out probably will imply a loss of concentration, because they will never allow themselves the luxury of more than a single here or a 2 there. However other batsmen might take the view that they've got their eye in and that they are going to try and dominate the bowling. If you get out to an aggressive shot then it's not necessarily lack of concentration, though it may be, but it could be poor shot selection. Your intention was probably right, your basic theory and thinking about the game was probably correct, it's just the execution that let you down.'

If it was not difficult enough for a batsman to focus his attention on the right things, his task is made even harder by the opposition's attempts to distract him. In years past these distractions might have been of a more gentlemanly nature than they are now, but as the financial stakes have risen, along with people's tolerance levels for these practices, all kinds of putting off tactics have become institutionalized into international cricket. The 1985 Australian touring team to this country was generally considered to be one of the friendliest and best-mannered of recent years; it also lost the Test series by 3 matches to 1. The lesson that Allan Border, the captain, drew from this was that charm does not pay. When he returned to England as captain of the 1989 touring team he had decided on a policy of non-fraternisation. Sledging levels reverted to the heyday of the Chappell era, the team were equally as surly off the field, and they convincingly won the Test series 4-0. No present day international team can plead innocence to the charge of sledging, though the England side is probably less guilty than most. The Australians have traditionally topped the league table, though Pakistan must now be edging them close. The Australians feel that the West Indies are past masters, while one can confidently expect the South Africans, once they find their international voice again, to be up there with the best of them. On an individual world ranking, Moin Khan, the Pakistani wicket-keeper, would find himself near the top if the voting was conducted by the English batsmen who played against him last summer.

Apart from international cricket being a harder and nastier game than before, what this shows is that teams believe that sledging and other forms of distraction are successful tactics, or why else would they continue to bother? No batsman would reach Test level without a proven ability to concentrate over the period of an innings. Therefore, the theory must go, if the batsman is unlikely to be distracted from his objective if left to his own devices, it is up to the fielding side to help him to lose concentration.

While there may be no substitute for time in the middle as the way to learn how to bat for four or five hours, there are a number of techniques that a batsman can learn to prevent himself being distracted. Most psychologists agree that basic methods of concentration training, such as asking people to tick off randomly situated numbers in order, are of limited application in sport, because most performers lose concentration due to external stimuli such as the noise of a large crowd and the chatter of the opposition. Instead, what Graham Jones recommends is simulation training whereby a performer is faced with a situation in which he habitually loses concentration and learns to handle it differently. It is this method that he employed to great effect in his work with Lisa Opie, the squash player. 'Lisa was renowned throughout the game as a woman who could not contain her frustration when things were going wrong. Her opponents knew this and would deliberately try to get her riled so that she would lose her concentration and with it the game. It got so bad that in one match at Wembley during the British Open she started arguing with the umpire when she was given a bad call and got so angry that she threw her racket out of the court. It flew just past the umpire's head; she said it was an accident, but the incident got her banned for six months. During our work together we would set up situations in practice games where the score would be close and the umpire would give bad calls. This way she could experience going through the frustration; eventually she learnt how to keep her concentration by accepting bad calls and modifying her behaviour accordingly.'

The implications of this for cricket are apparent. A batsman who finds sledging disturbing can turn it to his advantage. He doesn't do this by pretending that it doesn't bother him, but by acknowledging that it does, and telling himself that the reason that the fielding side is sledging him is because they think he's a good batsman. He simultaneously authenticates his own experience, denies the opposition the reaction they want to provoke, keeps his concentration, and boosts his self-confidence.

Concentrating is hard work. The number of captains whose personal form has deteriorated when called upon to attend to more than just their batting is testament to that. Many have found that the demands of planning on field tactics, taking care of the players, and talking to the media, have left them mentally exhausted by the time they take guard in the middle. Even captains who appear to cope with the extra responsibility have a breaking point. Graham Gooch had publicly voiced his doubts about leading the England side to India last winter long before he decided to go, and hindsight shows that his intuition was probably right.

The frequency of international fixtures, and the spotlight under which they are played, means that more demands are being made on Test cricketers. Given that most international batsmen have high concentrational skills, the players that prove to have the longest careers in the future may well be those who can best protect themselves from mental fatigue by switching off at the end of the day's play. The traditional form of evening entertainment for most cricketers is a drink or three, and very nice it is too. However as any doctor or psychologist will tell you, drinking is not the best way to relax, because it slows down one's reactions and decision making. Techniques like breath control are preferable alternatives. In the end one may even find that those batsmen who can incorporate the most effective relaxation techniques into their routine are those with the mental stamina to concentrate hardest at the crease.

ROBIN'S STORY

Concentration is the art of recognising what one's challenge is at any given moment and being able to focus exclusively on it, which isn't as easy as it sounds. As the bowler is running in, the aim is to pay attention to the bowler and to be oblivious to everything else. It doesn't always happen that way. There are times when people wander in front of the sight screens and I pull away because I've been distracted. I get annoyed with myself when this happens since it shows me that I'm not properly focused. What's happening 100 yards away is really not my concern. There are probably just as many occasions when people move around behind the bowler's arm and I don't notice because I'm concentrating on the right things.

Each bowler presents a different challenge and so what I focus my attention on as he runs in can vary greatly. A batsman must know what each bowler is capable of doing with the ball. A bowler like Aqib Javed isn't quick enough to bounce me out so I would be thinking about getting further forward to him than to someone like Curtley Ambrose. Likewise if I get four inswingers in a row from a bowler I am not automatically on the look out for an outswinger because I might know that he is incapable of delivering it. On the other hand if it was someone like Phil Newport, who can move the ball both ways, then I most definitely would. It's when the bowler gets into his delivery stride that I begin to get a better idea of what sort of delivery to expect. If he bowls from wide of the crease I can assume that the ball will be an inswinger; if he comes in close to the stumps I expect the outswinger. If his left shoulder dips then the ball will be short, while if the bowler stays in a more upright position it will be of a much fuller length. I suspect that often the bowler doesn't have a clue how much a particular delivery will deviate off line, if at all, so I don't make up my mind about what shot to play until the ball is bowled. Going through the options doesn't mean that I can guarantee to play the right shot but it does mean that I am rarely taken by surprise.

Part of the process is for the batsman to be able to put himself in the bowler's position. For instance, if a spinner drops a ball short and you cut him for four, you can be fairly certain that the next ball will be pitched further up because he'll collect a few angry looks from his captain and his colleagues if it isn't. So there is a good chance that he will over-compensate and give you something which you will be able to drive.

I've often thought that it's no coincidence that some of the world's most successful bowlers like Ian Botham, Imran Khan, Kapil Dev, Malcolm Marshall, and Richard Hadlee are all-rounders because knowing how it feels to be a batsman gives them a distinct advantage. Even someone like Dennis Lillee, who was only really considered as a bowler, developed into a reasonably competent batsman as he learnt to think like one, and his bowling improved as a result. Concentration is vital for a bowler, too, and many of them don't think enough about what they are doing. Of course they know where a batsman has a weakness, and that the best line is six inches outside the off stump, but they don't get any further than that. Cricket is a waiting game and the bowler and the batsman must be able to curb their feelings of frustration. Too often bowlers let batsmen off the hook by losing their patience and with it their concentration. It's easy to see how it happens; bowling is hard work, many pitches are prepared as batting wickets, and a batsman playing and missing can be the last straw. A bowler who repeatedly beats the bat is usually tempted to try an inswinger to upset the batsman, when what the batsman is really worried about is receiving the similar ball to the one that beat him. More often than not the attempted inswinger will be off line and end up as a leg stump half-volley which the batsman can clip to the boundary. All the hard work that the bowler has put in has gone to waste, and the batsman has been given the upper hand on a plate. It can take a long time for bowler's to learn this, and it's one reason why spinners do better as they get older. Their technique hasn't necessarily improved but their concentration has. Unfortunately many fast bowlers' physiques give out before they grasp this, but those that can stay fit, like Richard Hadlee, can take a phenomenal amount of wickets later in their careers.

It goes without saying that a batsman must be aware of the field settings and be alert to any changes in the placements, because by doing so you can weigh up the risk factor attached to any shot and work out where you are going to score your runs. Where fielders aren't positioned can tell you as much about a bowler's plan of attack as where they are. A captain doesn't leave gaps in the field merely because he hasn't got enough fielders to block every shot; from time to time he will leave a gap deliberately. Whenever Malcolm Marshall is bowling big inswingers he tends to leave a big gap in the covers because he wants to tempt the batsman into driving at him. I was deceived by this ploy myself in a tour match in the West Indies, and Malcolm has never let me forget it.

Frustration is one of a batsman's greatest enemies. When you're not timing the ball well or the bowler is not giving you anything to score from, it's important not to lose concentration by trying to hit your way out of trouble. Having a slog might work 10% of the time, but the rest it won't. Whenever I'm scratching around unable to get the ball anywhere near the middle of the bat, I try to remind myself to play my way out of trouble by going back to basics. I tell myself that I'm not playing well, so I must concentrate on maintaining my technique and staying calm. If I haven't got the timing to hit boundaries I can at least keep the scoreboard ticking over by looking for the ones and twos, so I will focus on where I can sneak a few singles. It's a good tactic in a Test match, but it's a critical one for a limited overs game. Picking up an extra run per over for a period of 20 overs can make the difference between winning and losing the game, and besides which, nothing infuriates a bowler more than a sharp single. He will have bowled what he thinks to be a dot ball, and yet he will look up at the scoreboard to find another run added to his analysis. He will probably give the fielder a hard stare, the fielder will glower back, and team morale will be sapped, when in fact it was nobody's fault. It was just a good run. With any luck the bowler will be so annoyed by it that he won't be thinking hard enough about what he is doing with his next delivery and give you a chance to score again.

One of the best examples of a player keeping his concentration when he was playing badly that I have ever witnessed was Graham Gooch's 2nd innings against the New Zealanders in Auckland in early 1992. Graham scored 114, and he wasn't just bad, he was atrocious. He was playing as poorly on 114 as he was on 0, yet it didn't bother him. Goochie would either play and miss or hit the ball for four. There was no in between, and poor Danny Morrison must have been tearing his hair out wondering what he had to do to get him out. We were killing ourselves with laughter at Goochie's ineptitude, but it was a remarkable innings. Most batsmen would have given their wicket away at 20, assuming they had survived that long, but Graham was so mentally strong that he could forget about the bad shots and go on to notch up another Test century.

Some people have claimed that an excess of one-day cricket has given rise to poor technique in the longer versions of the game, but I feel that this is the stock excuse for playing poor cricket. A batsman has to be able to focus on what he's doing and to discipline himself accordingly. If I find myself playing the wrong shot at the wrong time it's because I'm not concentrating properly. The technique should be the same for a cover drive or a square cut whatever the game. There's little difference for me between a one-day and a Test innings when I first go out to bat, because in both cases I'm trying to play straight. Batsmen get out just as often by not playing straight in a limited overs game as they do in a Test. I realize that I have an advantage of either opening or batting at number three, and that Neil Fairbrother and Mark Ramprakash might have to chance their arm a little sooner when coming in lower down the order, but not as often as one might think. Usually it's only in the last 5-10 overs that you need to think about having a real slog; before that you can play relatively orthodoxly. Of course there are times when the team's position in a one-day game demands that I take some chances, so then I might start to hit the ball in the air, but by and large I will aim to keep the ball on the ground. If you mistime a ball along the ground the worst that can happen is that you don't get a run, whereas if you mistime a ball in the air the chances are you're out.

The reason why so many batsmen get out to poor shots in one-day cricket again comes down to frustration. You can feel that the run rate is getting out of hand and that desperate measures are called for long before they are. It's happened to me before now, and I dare say that it will happen again. When it does it's crucial that I concentrate on what the demands of the situation really are. This is where it can be helpful to talk to one's partner. You can work out together where and when the runs are going to come from. The Pakistanis tend to bowl a much better length towards the end of the innings: so against them I would try to accelerate the innings sooner than against the West Indians who give you more to hit in the last few overs. The important thing is not to panic. I like to think that I can score my runs as quickly as anyone, so if I'm struggling then there's a fair chance that others will struggle too. Therefore it's pointless having a slog and getting out, thereby bringing a new batsman to the wicket who hasn't got his eye in, unless the situation really is that bad. In the long run you're more likely to win a tight game if one of your main batsmen is still there at the death. I'm not a selfish player and if we ended up losing the game by a few runs I would hope that people wouldn't say: 'Robin Smith lost us the game' but that I did well to get us so close to our target.

There are times when I fail to concentrate simply because I am too relaxed. Relaxation is an integral part of batting because it's impossible to concentrate for long periods of time without it. I aim to switch off once the ball has gone dead or I'm certain of what is going to happen next, but I can get it wrong. My run out in the first innings of the Test against the West Indies at Headingley in 1991 was totally attributable to a loss of concentration. I had hit the ball wide of third man and I was so sure that there were two runs to be had, that I forgot there is a huge slope running down the ground toward the Football Stand end and that the ball was travelling much faster over the outfield than normal. Curtley Ambrose threw in a superb return and I was out by inches. This lapse in concentration was made worse by the fact that I was batting well at a time when the team was in some trouble and I quite needlessly made our position worse.

Another problem with switching off between deliveries is remembering to pay attention to the next one. This is a major cause of wickets falling after a break in play. In the first Test against the West Indies in Jamaica in 1990 I was batting with Allan Lamb to try and build a winning platform. Lamby was batting at his best, and I was merely supporting him by giving him as much of the strike as possible. There was no pressure on me to score fast and we were going along nicely together up until a drinks break. The first ball after the resumption I played a wild shot against Bishop and was caught at slip. I was tired having batted for a long time in the heat and I paid the price for not being able to re-focus my attention quickly enough.

There are times when over-confidence affects my concentration. After my first two Tests against the West Indies in 1988 I was looking forward to the game against the Sri Lankans at Lord's since it seemed to be the ideal opportunity to fill my boots with runs against some friendly bowling and to secure my place on the winter tour to India. I had played for Hampshire against the Sri Lankans on a number of occasions and had always done well. In one match I had scored a 100 and a 96 in the same game, and had only missed the second century because I was going for a big hit in an effort to reach the fastest hundred of the season, so I was hoping for at least 70 in the first innings. I became so eager to dominate the bowling that I played a ridiculously ambitious shot to a wide full toss and dragged the ball back on to my stumps for 31. I didn't make the same mistake in the second innings; when I went out to bat England only needed a few runs to win their first Test for a long time, and I was determined to be there at the end no matter how long it took.

Under-estimating the opposition is an easy mistake to make. Most county teams have one bowler, usually the overseas signing, who is a bit better than the rest, but it is fatal to relax one's attention when he is taken off. A lot of people in this country couldn't understand how relatively unknown bowlers like Latham, Harris, and Larsen, did so well for New Zealand in the World Cup. The fact is that they were the ideal bowlers for low, slow wickets. If they had played at the WACA they would have been murdered, but in New Zealand the most effective bowlers in one-day cricket are those that bowl wicket to wicket at medium pace. Batsmen didn't want to show these bowlers respect but they earned it because they were so hard to get away.

A loss of concentration isn't always as obvious as a poor shot. You can play what might be a perfectly reasonable shot in some circumstances, but in another situation it can be the wrong one. Against fast bowlers that generate a lot of bounce I try to play most of my back foot shots with a parallel bat, because if the ball bounces more than I expect there's a much better chance of an edge going over the top of the slips or of missing it altogether than if I play with a vertical bat. At Trent Bridge in 1990 I played a back foot drive off Courtney Walsh that would have been fine on another wicket or against someone of less pace but I forgot about the bounce in the pitch and was caught at slip.

Generally speaking I'm happy with my attitude towards the game, but there has been the odd occasion when I've known that I'm not going to be able to concentrate properly even before I go out to bat. It hasn't happened at a Test match because the pressure is sufficient to focus my attention at least until I'm settled into my innings, but it has happened when I've been playing for Hampshire. I've mentioned that towards the end of last season I found it hard to maintain my enthusiasm for county cricket. By the time we played Essex we had been away from home for a fortnight and no matter how hard I tried to talk myself into wanting to do well, I still felt flat. I realized I was going to struggle to concentrate at the crease so I decided to go out to bat without a helmet. I thought that if nothing else was going to make me pay attention the prospect of serious injury might. If there's one thing that's guaranteed to irritate a fast bowler it's the sight of a batsman without a helmet because he sees it as an insult to his manhood, and immediately I went out to bat Mark Ilott began to bowl a great deal quicker. He can be quite difficult to pick because he's got the left armer's ability to deliver a short ball with a flick of the wrist rather than a coil of the body, and he let go a bouncer that I shaped to pull, missed, and the ball shot past my head. I knew that it had been a close call because I had heard the air whistle as the ball went by, and as I turned to look at Goochie in the slips I could see a look of terror in his eyes. I should have called for a helmet after that, and I got very snappy when some of my Hampshire colleagues suggested that I did, but I had far too much pride. I wouldn't recommend batting without a helmet to anyone else as a cure for wandering concentration because it can be dangerous, but it certainly kept me on my toes, and I'm sure I batted for longer than I would have done otherwise.

One of the best features of county cricket is that for the most part it is played in good spirit. You don't get the sledging and other tactics that teams use to make a batsman lose concentration in international cricket. A fast bowler might let off steam and say a few words if someone plays and misses a couple of times, but that's as far as it goes. Everyone plays hard, but nothing too personal is ever said. County cricket is a small world; we play each other so often that we get to know one another quite well, and if you do have a problem with another player it's easier to sort it out over a drink rather than risk spoiling the atmosphere of a match and getting a bad reputation for yourself.

I did have some experience of sledging before I played Test cricket, because it could hardly have been otherwise playing in the same Currie Cup side as Mike Procter, one of the all-time great sledgers. Even so, I was surprised and depressed by what I discovered at international level. My first real taste of how unpleasant it can be came against the Australians in 1989. It wasn't just the sledging that got to me, but their arrogant attitude. Before that series I had idolized Allan Border, because he was a symbol of what could be achieved through dedication, and whenever Australia was playing a Test match I used to turn to his score first. It meant a lot to me to be playing against him, and I found it very upsetting that he behaved in the way that he did towards me. Perhaps I took it all too personally, but I was new to international cricket, I am a sensitive person, and it's not the way I like to play the game. It's hard to say that the sledging affected my form because I averaged in the mid 60s for that series, but it certainly got to me. Maybe if their bowlers had given me more trouble then it would have been more important to maintain my total concentration.

Not all teams go in for sledging. One of the reasons that I've always enjoyed playing the West Indians is that they have a good attitude towards the game. Sure there are the odd heated moments such as at Trinidad between Lamb, Stewart, and Haynes, and at Barbados between Greenidge and Small but these are minor

115

incidents that are quickly forgotten by the players. Even so attitudes in Test cricket have hardened. Early on in Allan Lamb's career players like Dennis Lillee and Jeff Thomson would have a go at the batsman on the field, and a laugh and a drink with him off it. The present Australian side won't even do that. Lamby and I wandered into the Australian dressing-room to have a drink with them at the end of a day's play at Brisbane in 1990, and we got a frosty reception. It was so uncomfortable that we drank our beer in record time and left as soon as we could. On the way out Lamby turned to me and said: 'That's the last bloody time I ever go into their dressing-room.'

The more Test cricket that I've played, the more I've got used to these unsettling tactics, and for the most part they don't distract or disturb me any more. However the Pakistani team that toured England last year made the Australians look like saints, and there is no doubt that at times I did let them get to me, and my concentration suffered. At least with the Australians the abuse only came from about half the team and there was the odd lull, but with the Pakistanis it was relentless. Winning was the only thing that mattered to them, and anything to break the batsman's concentration was considered fair game. Close fielders would move around a little and chatter to each other when Mushtaq was bowling. At times I had to pull away as the bowler ran in and invite the fielders to finish their conversation. Javed Miandad would affect innocence and make some reference to the umpire about the over rate. We knew what was going on but it was hard to ignore it. The only time when the talking subsided was at the Oval, but they were so dominant in that match that there wasn't much need for it.

Ideally I would have been able to shrug it off and not be affected, but I was hurt and angry with what went on; I allowed myself to be distracted, and so you could say that the Pakistani tactics paid off. Barry Richards once said to me that the way to deal with a bowler who was giving you a verbal barrage was to look him in the eyes and say nothing. The bowler is the one that has to turn away and walk back to his mark, and because it's him that breaks the gaze the batsman has the psychological advantage. Unfortunately I was unable to do that with Waqar. Still, towards the end of the series it seemed as though even some of the Pakistanis had got fed up with the on-field hostilities. As I walked out to bat in the last one-day international at Old Trafford Waqar gave me the usual welcome and I was about to give him a piece of my mind in return when Wasim Akram said: 'Why don't the pair of you just make up; you're beginning to piss me off.' A lot of my friends expressed surprise that I shook Waqar's hand at the presentations after that game, and, although it was an instinctive gesture on my part, I'm glad I did, because I don't like holding grudges. Besides, in some ways I have something for which to thank him; my attitude and concentration were tested to the limit and I came though intact, which in the long run can only make me stronger both as a person and as a cricketer.

Comparing different players' powers of concentration is almost impossible. Allan Border's Test average is about 7 runs per game better than David Gower's, which is a huge gulf and certainly not one that accurately reflects their relative levels of ability. Though I can't prove it, this indicates to me that Gower wasn't as focused as Border. Gower probably lost concentration ten times in his Test career when he could either have remained not out or scored a great many more runs, in which case his average might have been on a par with Border's. On the other hand, is Graeme Hick's concentration any better than his Worcester team mates who don't score as many runs as he does? It may be, but one reason Graeme goes on to score so many big hundreds is that he gets his runs so quickly. He is such a fine striker that his average time for the first 100 must be about three hours, and the second will be even faster than that. So he can score 170 in the time it takes Tim Curtis to reach 100, and yet both efforts require the same level of application.

As far as my own levels of concentration are concerned, I'm aware there is plenty of scope for improvement. I've talked of my weaknesses in this area and I think they show in my 50 to 100 conversion ratio at Test level. I've scored 20 fifties and only 8 hundreds. Some of the fifties have been not outs but even so the ratio should be much nearer to 2:1. Martin Crowe has a ratio that is close to 1:1. Having said that, I'm still proud of my record, and my performances against the West Indies show me that there isn't too much wrong. I was astonished to discover that in my comparatively short career I have played about the same number of innings against the West Indians as Mike Gatting. Allan Lamb, David Gower and Geoff Boycott have only played a handful more, and if one compiled a ranking of all batsmen based on the average length of time spent at the crease against the West Indians, I would be second.

Tiredness can make an enormous difference to one's concentration. You only have to be a little bit jaded for your attention to wander, allowing your mind to fill up with outside distractions and worries, and at Test level a momentary loss of concentration can be fatal. On tour it can be hard to get enough time to unwind, and get mentally ready for the next game. Everything happens at such a frantic pace. We're either travelling, practising, or playing. Touring teams are often the focus of a great deal of interest in foreign countries and everything we do comes under public scrutiny. Any free time that we do get tends to be spent with other members of the team, or with journalists staying in the same hotel, which is fun but not always relaxing.

Back to back Test matches are a killer. On the tour to the West Indies in 1990 there was only one day between the fourth Test in Barbados and the fifth in Antigua. I had batted for about six hours on the last day in Barbados, and I was in no mental or physical shape to play another Test so soon afterwards. I think it's no coincidence that I was pinned on the jaw for the first time in my career at Antigua. It wasn't just me that was exhausted; nearly all of us were. In fact the only person who definitely wasn't was Courtney Walsh who hadn't played in Barbados. He clearly thought that he had something to prove for having not been selected for the fourth Test. He bowled tremendously quickly, and turned out to be the difference between the two sides.

I'm learning the hard way that you have to manage your time properly as a Test cricketer. As I have become better known I have been asked to attend more and more events and dinners. My initial reaction up till now has always been to accept because it's nice to be asked and I don't like letting people down, but I've realized that for the sake of my sanity I'm going to have to learn to say no. The crunch came at the end of last season after I'd been away for three weeks continuously; I came home exhausted and took it out on Kath. She said: 'Thank God there's only one
more game and then that's it for a couple of months', but I'd contrived to make September as busy as any other month and we had little time together at home as a family. Cricket is a tiring game, and there's no point in my always being the nice guy if it means I'm in no fit mental state in the middle. Every person needs time to themself away from their profession and their colleagues. Test cricketers need it more than most, so it's stupid not to make the best of the time I do have. Getting a balance between one's private and professional life can be tricky when you're in the public eye, and I haven't found it yet. Going out in the evening should make one's cricket more enjoyable, not less, and no one can pay attention at the crease if they are tired from a function they didn't want to go to the night before or are dreading the one to come.

People always tend to give loss of concentration as a reason for getting out, but sometimes you are dismissed simply because the bowler has bowled a great delivery. I was amazed to read in one paper after my innings of 96 at Lord's against Australia in 1989 that I had lost concentration when I was bowled by an inswinger from Terry Alderman. In fact the ball swung into me, and then moved away from the bat, up the slope, to hit the off stump. I may get out at times through not concentrating when I'm tired, over-confident, or distracted either by my thoughts or the opposition, but I can categorically state that when I was within four runs of my first Test century and was battling to save a Test against Australia in front of a full house at Lord's wasn't one of them.

CHAPTER SIX

ANXIETY AND FAILURE

Fear is one of the most basic emotions and underpins more human endeavour than most people care to admit. Over the course of history many countries have recognised this and have used it as an instrument of domestic social control, while the policy of nuclear deterrence adopted by the NATO and Soviet bloc countries was predicated on a mutual fear of Armageddon. Fear can be a productive driving force; as an emotion stimulated by the threat of danger it is an essential part of human survival. A person who is outnumbered by attackers will find he has previously unknown resources of speed and endurance as he attempts to escape. Some fears, such as of extreme pain, are universal, even though people may experience them on different levels of intensity, depending on how naturally highly-strung or laid back they are. But not all threats are as straightforward. What may represent danger to one person may not to another. Some people are frightened of the dark; some people fear being ostraciZed for doing well, while others fear being teased for doing badly. What matters is not what a person is afraid of, but how well he copes with that fear. Problems only occur when it dominates an area of a person's life and prevents him from fulfilling his potential.

Graham Jones writes in his article 'Stress and Anxiety in Sport' that: 'an individual's emotional response is the result of an interaction between the individual and the environment. Stress is viewed as a stimulus which is present in the form of demands placed upon the individual by the environment.' Therefore, how fearful or anxious a sportsman becomes either prior to, or during, competition is liable to be determined by how stressful he perceives the demands that are made on him to be, and how well he copes with that stress. In some circumstances the performer will welcome the stress and use it to his advantage; the adrenalin buzz can give him an added edge that he could never find in training. In others he will feel overwhelmed, become anxious, and his self-confidence, motivation, and concentration will be affected. How positively or negatively a performance will be approached often depends as much on how the sportsman fared on the previous occasion that he found himself in the same situation, as on any inherent personality trait. This explains the apparent madness behind Robin Smith's preference for facing the likes of Ambrose, Bishop, and Walsh on a bouncy Sabina Park wicket, rather than Kumble, Raju, and Chauhan, on a crumbling Madras turner.

There are three forms of fear in a sporting context; there is the fear of physical injury or death, the fear of failure, and the fear of success. In some sports the former isn't an issue. There have been no recorded snooker fatalities, the only physical risk that darts offers is alcohol poisoning, while the only thing that anyone will be dying of at a bowls match is boredom. The risk of injury is nowhere near as great for a batsman as, say, a racing driver but it is real nevertheless. George Summers died four days after being hit on the head by a short ball while batting for Nottinghamshire against the MCC at Lord's in 1870, and Nari Contractor and Ewan Chatfield wouldn't have wanted to come a great deal closer.

Batsmen devise their own psychological methods for dealing with pace bowling. Mike Brearley hummed Beethoven quartets to himself when Michael Holding was running into bowl. 'It started off as a subconscious reaction, but at a certain point I began to do it deliberately. Holding had a mesmerising affect on me, and I found that by humming a tune that I found rich and pleasant, I was less anxious and frightened. It was almost like being in another world, and as long as I heard the tune in my head I knew I would see the ball all right.'

All batsmen have an enthusiasm threshold for fast intimidatory bowling, and for some the fear of injury induces a state akin to shell-shock. Mike Denness took such a psychological battering at the hands of Lillee and Thomson on the Ashes tour of 1974 that he had to drop himself from the Test side. Given the real and

122

imagined fear of injury one might ask why it took so long for batsmen to take adequate measures to protect themselves. Mike Brearley was one of the first to furnish himself with a helmet. 'It was a difficult decision to take, partly because I was worried about what other people might think, and partly because my own attitude towards it was ambivalent. On the one hand it made perfect sense, and on the other I thought: 'What a jerk.' Brearley's fear of what others might think was well-founded among ex-players who no longer put their heads on the line, but elsewhere he received support from surprising quarters. 'I would have expected Rod Marsh to have dismissed the helmet as namby-pamby, but his only criticism was that it should have been bigger.'

Within a few years Mike Brearley's stance was vindicated as the world's greatest batsmen took up the helmet, and nowadays one can count on one hand the Test batsmen, like Viv Richards and Richie Richardson, who eschew its use. But if the threat of death has been eliminated, the possibility of physical injury remains. Despite the best protection that science can offer, a batsman can expect severe bruising and the odd broken bone at some point in his career. How much a batsman is affected by this will depend in part on his perceptions of pain. One reason Brian Close was so successful against fast bowling was that he considered losing his wicket to be infinitely more painful than getting hit. The bruises he collected from being peppered with bouncers were no more than an everyday hazard of the job. However, despite outward appearances to the contrary, it's not the batsman's bones that the bowler is really interested in breaking, but his nerve.

Grayson Heath frequently stresses the importance of time in cricket, and it is crucial in understanding a batsman's anxiety. Many sportsmen report that they get anxious before an event, but that once it has started the nerves disappear because they are so involved in the activity that there isn't time to think about their anxiety. A batsman has more than enough time to worry and so the stress can increase; he doesn't have the luxury of physical exercise to take his mind away from his fears between each delivery of an over; the only company he has is the voices inside his head. His only compensation is that the longer he spends at the wicket the more likely that his anxiety will recede, as time spent in crease occupation will imply a level of competence in dealing with whatever his fears may be.

Failure for a batsman is total and absolute. A footballer may miss a penalty but he will remain on the field of play and have a chance to redeem himself; a golfer may miss an easy putt but there will always be the next hole to make amends. There are no second chances for a batsman when the umpire's finger goes up, and he may take no further part in the match for a couple of days. So part of the game is for the batsman to learn to accommodate this. Ideally a batsman will recognize that making mistakes is part of his growth as a cricketer, and that just as success does not bring true happiness, failure shouldn't bring total misery. But this is no easy thing for a batsmen to accept, and his response to getting out will vary enormously; if he thinks he's played well, scored a decent amount of runs, and that he was out to a good ball rather than to a poor shot, he won't be too upset. If he's been given out for a low score, or worse still has had a run of low scores, he would want the ground to swallow him up. Failure is very public, and the bigger the occasion and the larger the crowd, the greater the sense of failure. A batsman's own private humiliation is related to the thought of other people watching, and his public humiliation is related to his own sense of shame at having failed. Players react in different ways to this. Some have no problem showing their despair and disappointment, others feel the need to walk off as if losing their wicket was of little concern, and there is a third group who will try to deny the reality of their experience by always claiming that they were given out unjustly.

Chris Smith feels that the present county championship structure allows players to accept failure too easily, with the result that many are inexperienced in dealing with their anxieties on the big occasions. 'You get four or five innings each week playing county cricket, so the feeling that if you don't do well today then there will be another chance tomorrow is always in the back of many players' mind. I think it's meant that batsmen sometimes think 'Ah what the hell' and give their wicket away when they come across a big fast nasty bowler who they don't fancy facing. In South Africa, where Robin and I played most of our cricket in our early days, each innings was much more precious, and we learned to take full advantage of every opportunity we were given. There would be a Currie Cup game every three weeks, and in between we would only get one innings per week playing for our club side at weekends. What made matters worse was that Natal has a sub-tropical climate which ensured that most pitches were a seamers' paradise, and so a batsman's likelihood of failure was quite high. As a result, Robin and I had no choice but to learn to come to terms with our fear of failure early on in our careers. It's not something that goes away, but you can get used to coping with it.'

The fear of success - 'choking' when on the verge of achievement - is well documented in the sporting world. There are golfers who have missed the vital putt to win a championship, and tennis players who lose when in a seemingly unbeatable position. It's hard to put one's finger on the reasons for 'choking'. Clearly it is closely allied to the fear of failure; what greater failure can there be than to lose something that you looked like winning? Yet psychologists have also pointed to the trauma of attainment, and this has to be the explanation for success phobia in cricket. Many batsmen play fluently throughout an innings yet become nervously becalmed when in sight of a landmark such as a century. It cannot be because there is a risk of failure, because coming second or failing is a meaningless concept to a batsman in the 90s. Logically speaking, scoring 90 is a success by any standards.

Anxiety can make apparently rational human beings behave and think in decidedly illogical ways. It's hard to contemplate a more lucid intelligent cricketer than Mike Brearley, but even he admits to some bizarre thought processes. 'I was always frightened of the opposition's best bowler, no matter who he was. If we were playing against a Surrey side that included both Geoff Arnold and

Robin Jackman I'd feel much more relaxed facing Jackman, because he was the lesser bowler. Yet if Geoff Arnold wasn't playing, I would become anxious about Robin Jackman. It was as if I always needed to make one bowler the fearful one.' Chris Smith believes that such twisted logic has prevented Robin from scoring as many runs as he should at county level. 'I'm sure that at the back of Robin's mind is the sub-conscious idea that there is a finite number of runs that he can score. He thinks that if he gets too many for the county there won't be enough in the bank for the Test matches, and so he backs off slightly.'

It is during a Test match that a batsman is liable to feel at his most anxious, because it is there that the greatest demands are placed on him, and there is the greatest risk of making a fool of himself. Despite not having the international career that he would have hoped for, Chris Smith feels that he came to terms with the stress of Test cricket. 'I was never an out and out certainty to be picked for the whole series or even the next game, and I realized from the very beginning that this was something I was going to have accept. Chris Tavare gave me some priceless help with this. He said: 'It's a great honour to play Test cricket for England, and I approach each game as if it was the last I was going to play. I simply go out and try to enjoy the occasion in its entirety.' I made an effort to adopt this policy and it worked for me. I was still nervous when I went out to bat, and I still worried about how much longer I would be playing for, but the edge was taken off my fear of failure, and I did enjoy the eight Tests I played. Too many players are only concerned with doing enough to stay in the side; they put so much pressure on themselves that they don't enjoy their cricket.'

A state of over-anxiety will, by definition, adversely affect a batsman's performance, but moderate levels of anxiety can be used to his advantage. As Graham Jones points out, it's not that top sportsmen don't experience the same intensity of anxiety as lesser performers but that they are better able to control those feelings and respond positively towards them. A batsman will want to have certain levels of anxiety before and during an innings. If used positively they can stimulate feelings of arousal and excitement; they will make him aware of the importance of what he is doing, make him guard against complacency, and remind him to keep his concentration. It's when the anxiety is perceived in a negative way, when he spends more time concentrating on what others are doing, he is paralysed into indecision in his shot making, and his self-confidence is affected, that the batsman is in trouble.

The difference between the two approaches is something that can only really be gauged by the batsman himself. Many observers are fond of saying that Robin Smith is a nervous starter, but can they really tell from what they see? Sure, he bounces around a great deal at the crease, but does that make him any more anxious than someone who stands still with a deadpan expression, or does it just mean that he has found a different way of coping? It may well be that sometimes he is coping better than others, but his results would certainly indicate that he deals with his anxiety reasonably well.

Psychologists differentiate between cognitive and somatic anxiety – the mental and the physical. Cognitive anxiety, characterized by negative expectations, tends to appear much earlier prior to competition than the physical 'butterflies in the stomach' or feelings of nausea. It is important for a batsman to understand how each affects him, because only then can he take the appropriate action. It is generally held that cognitive anxiety best responds to mental relaxation techniques, such as meditation, mental rehearsal and visualization, while the somatic responds to muscular relaxation techniques, such as tensing and relaxing different muscle groups in turn, and breath control. Such techniques can take some time to learn, but once learnt can be effective in a matter of seconds. The benefits are obvious. If the batsman can control his body to prevent the onset of muscular tension, he may go a long way to removing those technical faults caused by moving in a stiff, jerky manner. Also, as we have seen, the vital question is not the intensity of the batsman's anxiety, but whether his feelings are congruent with the way he would ideally like to feel, and these techniques give him the means to achieve this. Of course, no batsman will have exactly the same anxiety feelings before each innings, nor will he necessarily want to do so, and it's unrealistic to imagine that he will be able to match the two perfectly each time. Even so it is clear that those batsmen who analyze their anxieties and learn how to control them best are those who are better equipped to deal with the stress of first-class cricket.

ROBIN'S STORY

I believe that people are born with different amounts of fear and courage. As a child I wasn't physically afraid of anything. I would swim in water that was way out of my depth, surf in areas that weren't protected by shark nets, and even though I've only had three fights in my life, and have been hurt in all three, I would have been prepared to brawl with anyone if necessary. During my rugby career I wasn't frightened of anyone, though the fact that I was larger than everyone else may have had something to do with it, and ever since I began to play cricket I've never been afraid of fast bowling. I could face the bowling machine for hours on end in the garden at home, getting a growing sense of excitement from seeing how fast I could turn it up and still cope.

Even today, I don't really mind if I get hit by the ball, providing I don't break a bone which would sideline me for a few months. Of course it stings for a while if you get hit on the inside of the thigh or on the chest, but I've found that I can switch off my mind to the pain. I much prefer batting without any body armour, and it's only if we're playing on a bouncy wicket and there is a genuine risk of getting injured that I will wear a chest guard. Even then I will wear the protection, more to ensure that I don't let the side down by getting injured and being unable to bat, than out of any concern for my personal safety. I've been hit on the helmet twice and have had my right index finger broken, but I don't think these blows have had any effect on the way I bat. I haven't changed the way I play against the short ball, and while I have had extra padding put in my batting glove to protect my weaker finger, I've never shied away or found myself pulling my hand away from the bat.

I relish the challenge of fast bowling. I'm sure that many people would imagine that my most memorable piece of batting would be when I reached a century or won a match, but in fact it's the four or five overs before tea in the second innings of the Antigua Test in 1990. It's the only one of my innings that I've ever wanted to keep on video, though needless to say I've mislaid it. Lamby was either blocking Baptiste or hitting him for four, so I got stuck at Ian Bishop's end. Of the 14 balls I received, 13 were bouncers. I got hit on the body a few times, but it was unbelievably exhilarating. My Mum was in the stands, surrounded by West Indian fans baying for my blood, and she got so upset at seeing her darling little boy get knocked about that she burst into tears and had to leave. She bumped into Graham Otway, the *Today* cricket correspondent, behind the stands and told him: 'If this is what Test cricket is all about, then I'm not very interested in it.' I went into tea on 0 not out.

Shell-shock was a real problem before helmets were introduced, because it can have been no fun at all facing Lillee and Thomson on a bouncy Perth wicket with nothing to protect your head. Yet despite the clear-cut benefits of the helmet, I'm not convinced that wearing one hasn't made some batsmen a little careless. I'm sure that one reason why more and more batsmen get hit on the helmet is because they aren't really bothered if they get hit or not. It was comparatively rare for someone to get hit in the old days because they knew that if they did they would be off to hospital. Even with all the protection on offer, batsmen can still become tentative after they have been hit. My good friend Paul Terry struggled for a while after his arm was broken against the West Indies. In his case the problem was more that he didn't have the strength in his left arm than a mental one, but it's been slightly different for Mark Nicholas. He got hit by Gladstone Small in 1982 and I don't think he's ever been as good a player since. Gladstone was distinctly quick in those days – I would certainly have worn a helmet against him – but for some reason, maybe due to a touch of arrogance, Mark didn't bother and got struck on the head. Over the last couple of years he's become more confident again, but before that it always seemed to me that he was unsure of himself against the quicks.

In general though, I find it hard to understand people who are scared of fast bowling. Obviously one makes exceptions for players who aren't in the side for their batting. Phil Tufnell gives the appearance of being in control but he is one of the least confident people I know, and he is so petrified of the ball that he can't stop himself stepping towards square leg as the bowler runs in. But for anyone who bats higher up the order there is no real excuse for looking worried and hovering about on the back foot. Cricket is a hard game, and fast bowling is part and parcel of it. If you can't fight it out for yourself and the team, then you've got a problem. If you let a bowler sense for a moment that you're uncomfortable and uncertain against him he's won the psychological battle, and he's going to inundate you with as many short-pitched balls as he can get away with. You've got to be prepared to look the bowler in the eye and show no fear. One of the batsmen who does this best is Allan Lamb; what he lacks in technique, he makes up for in courage, and it's no coincidence that he's produced his best performances against the West Indies. When you're being bombarded by a non-stop battery of four fast bowlers, it's a fight the whole time, and for that you need guts and a big heart. One of the demands of Test cricket is that you have to face over after over of short-pitched bowling, and there's no point moaning about it.

I know this all sounds a bit gung-ho, and I might re-read this passage in a few years time and think: 'How could I have ever said that?' After I've had a few thousand more balls aimed at my head by the world's best bowlers, and with my eyesight and reflexes no longer what they were, I'll probably be stepping away and trying to cut everything along with the best of them! Even so I do think that things are easier now for a batsman than they've ever been. We have a great deal more protection by way of padding and helmets than players of twenty years ago, and the new bouncer law means that a batter has a much better chance of guessing in which half of the wicket the ball will pitch.

As anyone who has watched me bat against Mushtaq in the summer and against the Indians in the winter will know, it is the spinners that cause me the most concern. I'm the first to admit that my technique against the slow bowlers needs modifying, but I feel that I am beginning to make the necessary adjustments. The reasons I am more comfortable against pace are relatively straightforward; I'm not worried about getting hurt, and I've had a lot of practice at it. Before Mushtaq came to England last summer I'd never faced a world-class leg spinner so I'm not that surprised that it took me a few games to work out a strategy against him. Likewise, having played most of my cricket in South Africa and England, I had had no experience of under-prepared Indian wickets that turned sharply from the first day. I'm sure that the more practice I get against different types of bowlers in different conditions, the less anxious I will become.

For me, anxiety is related to what I am being asked to do. I'm probably one of the noisiest blokes in the dressing-room, but if I'm asked to talk in a formal setting I get nervous because I don't think I'm any good at it. Even at a team talk I will get anxious if the skipper asks me if I've got anything to say. I've been asked to be best man five times, and on each occasion I was a gibbering wreck when I had to make the speech. After each speech I thought I had been a total disaster, and I needed Kath to reassure me that I had done OK. Last winter I decided that I needed to try to do something about this, because as I get better known I get more invitations to speak, and I don't want it always to be such an ordeal. I did a couple of question and answer sessions in local pubs, which I actually enjoyed, and hopefully as I get more practice I will become more confident.

Batting is a stressful occupation. My brother Chris says that he felt under greater pressure opening the batting for Hampshire day after day than he has ever felt as Chief Executive of the WACA where his decisions can cost a lot of money and jobs, and I'm happy to take his word for it. Luckily I enjoy the stress of batting; I like the feeling of putting myself under pressure and seeing how I will manage, but I do get anxious. Some batsmen like Viv Richards never seem to entertain a moment's uncertainty before they go out to bat, but I'm sure that even Viv must have the odd doubt from time to time, because it would seem unnatural not to. I know that Viv's a much more confident batsman than I am, but I suspect that part of his aloofness stems from a desire to hide any anxiety from the fielding side and to make the bowlers feel intimidated by his presence. Any batsman who walks slowly to the wicket with his shoulders hunched up gives the bowlers a lift, but at Test level I don't think that walking out purposefully has much effect on them because they are confident enough in their own ability anyway. The rituals that I go through, like waving my arms, blinking, and staring at the bowler, are designed to relax me rather than unnerve the opposition. Yet at county level it can be a little different; when you get someone like Graeme Hick marching out looking as if he means business before the other batsman has even left the field, you can see the bowlers get apprehensive. They know that if they can't get him out in the first quarter of an hour, the chances are he will tear them to shreds.

A lot of people assume that I'm an ultra nervous starter because of the way I jump up and down at the wicket, but I don't think this is necessarily so. Of course the stretching and jogging help me to calm my nerves and get rid of excess adrenalin, but I also do it because I'm often a little cold. I hate batting with a jersey on; if it's very chilly I will wear a short-sleeved sweater, but I'll never wear a long sleeved one. I'm sure that other batsmen get just as nervous as me but have less obvious ways of showing it. Mind you, if I was more nervous than anyone else it wouldn't bother me. All the top golfers say that the time to give up the game is when you lose your nervousness. If you can admit to yourself that you're nervous when you go out to bat and that you will probably play and miss a few times early on, it will be far less worrying when you actually do.

Being nervous isn't a problem as long as I can control it and make it work for me. Anxiety affects me in two ways - physically and mentally. It's hard to maintain the physical relaxation needed to play flowing rhythmical strokes when I'm over-anxious, and this can lead to technical faults. My timing comes from having my head and weight over the ball while playing the shot, but when I get too nervous I tense up and start pushing stiffly too early at the ball and end up either hitting it in the air or flashing at it outside the off stump.

Anxiety can also affect my judgement. Everyone should have a strategy for an innings before they go out to bat, but there are times when I find myself attempting shots that I had decided in advance not to play. I might have told myself always to play forward to a particular bowler unless the ball was very short, but at the critical moment uncertainty takes over and I don't move my feet at all. Every batsman wants to get the scoreboard moving and see runs against his name early in an innings, and if the runs don't flow it's easy to lose patience and play some stupid shots. You must remember that the bowlers you are facing deserve respect because they are the best in their country or county, but that they aren't machines and they will make mistakes. Everything about batting comes down to control - controlling your body and your emotions. Even though nerves affect me most at the beginning of an innings, I can lose control at any time. A bowler might run in and give me a bouncer which I hook for four. We might have a few words, he drops one short again, and I cut him to the boundary. By now the adrenalin will be pumping and there's a danger of letting passion take over by trying too ambitious a shot to the next ball.

It can be hard to relax yourself, especially during a big match when everything's buzzing. This is obviously a problem while I'm batting, and I have to deliberately calm myself down by taking deep breaths or giving myself a talking to, but it can also be difficult to switch off after a day's play when you know that you've got to be back out there again the next day. Linford Christie will only have four or five really important races each year, while footballers seldom have more than two matches lasting ninety minutes each per week, but Test players have up to sixty days of international cricket each year, not to mention countless crucial one-day and championship games for their counties.

Cricketers are fairly social animals, so when we're away from home, which we are a fair amount of the time, we tend to spend time together having a meal and a drink. I spend so much time worrying about and analyzing my game, that I find going out and having a laugh with a few friends the perfect antidote. My doctor would probably tell me that having a drink every night wasn't the best way to relax, but it seems to work for me, and besides, it's meant that I've never yet suffered from insomnia. When I'm at home I like to get away from cricket entirely, and spend time with my family. Kath and I have recently bought a new house near Salisbury which needs some work doing to it. I'm no DIY man, but I spend a lot of time thinking about it, and I am one of the world's best supervisors.

I've never had any great fear of success; I've never frozen on the big occasion or developed a psychological block about personal landmarks like my first Test fifty or hundred, but then I didn't have to wait that long to reach them. It's always been the fear of failure, of letting myself and my team mates down, that has made me anxious. Failure for a cricketer is written in black and white on the scorecard. Each innings you know that, unless you remain not out, you are going to make one mistake that will prove fatal, and the challenge is to make it later rather than sooner.

Everybody reacts differently to getting out, depending on the circumstances of their dismissal. David Gower is generally fairly composed, but I've seen him come in and throw his bat across the dressing-room. Some people walk in utterly devastated, place their bat down, and sit silently with their head in their hands, while others will come in and shout and scream for five minutes, and then will act perfectly normally. Getting out takes a while to sink in for me. I'll walk off quietly, say good luck to the next batter, and it will only hit me when I get to the dressing-room. It's often the little things like seeing someone padding up who would still be relaxing had I not been dismissed that gets to me first, and then I get furious with myself. Hopefully, after that it's all over. I tend not to throw my bat; I don't think Gray Nicholls would be too happy about replacing them the whole time, and I feel that most of the time my bat looks after me, and so the least I can do is to look after it in return.

There are times when you get one low score after another and everything seems to be going wrong. Then the aim is to remember that it happens to everyone, that you don't become a bad player overnight, that it's only a game, and that things will come right in the end. This is a hard attitude to maintain when cricket is your livelihood and your future depends on your success, but you have to learn to adopt it. I was devastated to be left out of the side for the first Test against Australia in 1989. I had realized after the tour to India had been cancelled that no one would be guaranteed a place in the Test side, but I'd started the season in fine form for Hampshire with four centuries, and I thought I'd done more than enough to ensure selection. It was a major setback when David phoned to say that I hadn't been picked. I was fairly calm over the phone and wished David and the team well, but deep down I was very depressed because I didn't see what else I could have done to get selected. Kath and I went to Lynmouth for a short break to get over the disappointment, and while we were there I bought a painting. It still hangs in the house today, and whenever I look at it I cast my mind back to how bleak I felt then. It reminds me that the bad times didn't last for ever then, and that there are always some good times round the corner. Most players can handle the good times, but the true mark of a class batsman is measured by how one gets through a bad patch. If you can survive with your self-belief and self-respect intact, you've mastered the game.

CHAPTER SEVEN

LUCK

Luck plays its part in all sports, but few games are so open to the vagaries of chance as cricket. Whether the umpire upholds a LBW or run out appeal, whether an involuntary edge goes to hand or just evades the fielder, whether a catch is accepted or not, or whether he gets the only ball of the day to deviate off line, are all out of the control of the batsman. The difference between playing and missing and getting an edge to the wicket-keeper can be a millimetre, but it can sometimes be the margin between success and failure of a career. Who will remember that a batsman played and missed on 0 if he goes on to a match-winning century, but who will forget if he finds the edge?

Over the course of a career one would expect the rub of the green to even out, but that still leaves the player to ponder each individual break, and some breaks are more damaging than others. Neil Fairbrother was mortified by his first experience of Test cricket. 'I was only 22 and I was making my debut in front of a packed home Old Trafford crowd against the Pakistanis. It had rained for much of the day, and so the extra hour rule came into operation. The nightwatchman was due to come in at 6.45, but sure enough a wicket fell at 6.42, and though we had some experienced batsmen still to come, I was pencilled in at 4 and I had to go out to bat. It was very dark and I lasted three balls, none of which found the middle of the bat. I found it desperately hard to bear. When I went to the bar after the day's play I felt as if I had let the whole world down. The three people who mean more to me than anyone else, my wife and my Mum and Dad, were there and I couldn't look them in the eye. I just wanted to go away and lie down on my own. I didn't get a knock in the second innings, and I was dropped for the next Test. So three balls facing someone who I would fancy taking runs off day in day out in a county game shaped the way I thought about Test cricket for a long time; it was too difficult, and I wasn't good enough. In fact it took me a good 18 months to come to terms with the fact that I wasn't a dumbo, and that I had a talent for the game.' There's no knowing whether perfect light would have made any difference, but one could hardly blame Fairbrother for thinking that the fates had conspired against him.

Chris Smith is another player whose Test career was blighted by ill-fortune. 'I played 7 of my 8 Tests in 1983/4 and the other in 1986, but I think that I was a much better player in the last four years of my career than when I was actually selected. I was certainly scoring as many runs in all types of cricket as Gooch and Hick, but I suspect I was still being judged on my performances of several years earlier. I also think that making my debut in the early eighties did my Test career no favours. Allan Lamb was already in the side, and when I was picked it meant that there were two South Africans in the side at a time when there was a lot of pressure being exerted on Lord's about South African players in the English team. Nowadays it's hardly given any consideration at all, as things have begun to change for the better politically.'

So what attitude should a batsman take to help him cope best? There are two ways that a player can attribute success and failure - internally and externally, and which one he chooses can affect his confidence. The internal is a reflection of skill level, and the external of luck. A player who attributes his success to his skill level can boost his self-confidence, while attributing failure to external factors need not dent his self-belief. Neil Fairbrother attributed his early failure at Test level internally, with disastrous consequences for his confidence, yet Chris Smith was able to preserve his self-belief after a shortened Test career by ascribing the causes externally.

The same process can be used for each dismissal. A batsman who says he got out to an unplayable delivery need have no fears that he was not good enough - it was merely his bad luck to receive such a ball. David Gower must have cursed his misfortune to be given out caught off his pad for 40 against the Indians in 1990 in the same innings that Graham Gooch notched up a triple century and Allan Lamb and Robin Smith both scored hundreds, but as long as he recognized it as bad luck there was no reason to doubt his ability. Of course batsmen can take this too far. Those who always believe they are the victims of an umpire's myopia, are in danger of not putting in sufficient effort to improve their skill levels.

Playing and missing raises some interesting problems of attribution. If the batsman thinks that the reason he is playing and missing is because he is batting like a wally then his confidence won't be improved, but if he attributes it to the bowler's skill then he won't undermine his belief in his ability. Yet if the batsman does attribute playing and missing to his skill level, he also has to acknowledge that luck is on his side because he is playing badly and getting away with it. With so many possibilities on offer, it is no wonder that David Gower suggests that the ideal approach is not to think about it. 'If you're in the right frame of mind you will forget about it. It doesn't matter if the shot you've played is an almighty swish which you know is the worst shot you've ever played, at least for twenty minutes, or whether you've been beaten by a good ball. As far as you're concerned you're not out and still in command, and as long as you maintain this belief you can play and miss as many times as you like. The basis for playing and missing is that it doesn't matter, and it's only pride that tells you it does. You can hit the next ball for four and invariably you do. The number of times this happens after a play and miss or a good shout is quite unbelievable.'

Just because a batsman attributes something internally or externally does not mean that that is the cause; it is just the way he has chosen to deal with his experience. Ideally a batsman will find a way to maximize his self-confidence whilst having a realistic appreciation of his skill levels. There are a lot of things a batsman can't control, so it's best to focus on the things he can. Over the course of a season he's bound to be given out LBW a number of times; the vast majority of decisions will be correct, and those that go against him will probably be counter-balanced by those that went in his favour. The batsman can't control those decisions; all he can do is to make sure he doesn't get hit on the pad. In the end, as Chris Smith says, luck is part of the game, and all you can do is get on with it. 'Cricket is all about coping with extreme levels of pressure, and luck is just part of it. If you can't cope you won't be any good at it. I can look back on my career and say in all honesty that I'm not disappointed. As far as I'm concerned I had my fair share of the brush of the grass.'

ROBIN'S STORY

Gary Player always used to say: 'The harder I practise, the luckier I get', and it's certainly worked out that way for me, too. I know that what he meant was that much of what other people mistake for luck is often the product of sheer hard work, but luck does play its part in cricket and I have found that there is a literal truth in what he said. I've always worked extremely hard at my game, and I feel that generally speaking the luck has gone my way. I've had a number of dodgy decisions go against me, but they've been matched by ones that have gone in my favour. Bad decisions have always been one of the hazards of the game, and I've made a point about not complaining about them, even if I've been angry about it at the time. Too many people are happy to accept a poor decision that counts in their favour, and make a song and dance about the ones that go against them.

The trouble with those decisions that work against you is that they always seem to come at the moments in your career when you feel that you can least afford them, when everything else seems to be going wrong as well. I don't know why this should be, but a lot of other players have had the same experience. I don't think it's just that one remembers the bad times more than the good. Maybe fortune really does favour the bold. When you're in a rich vein of runs you get more confident, you become more positive in your stroke play, and the luck starts running for you. I remember that I was short of runs and confidence going into the second Test against Australia at Melbourne in 1990. The first day of the match was on Boxing Day so there was a huge crowd and a great atmosphere, and there was no danger of a batsman losing concentration. The wicket was flat and true, and as David Gower proved, if you could get in and stay in there were big scores to be had. We lost Atherton and Gooch early on, but I felt in good nick from the word go. I had reached 30 when I was given out caught behind by Healy off Merv Hughes, and the umpire must have been the only person in the ground who actually believed I had hit the ball. Who knows what would have happened had the catch not been given? If I had gone on to make a decent score my confidence might have come back, and the tour might have turned out differently. As it was, I regarded that 30 as a failure, and when I was out to a dreadful shot in the second innings, the pressure that I was under seemed to intensify considerably.

There have been other times when I've felt that my career could do with a little injection of good fortune to give it an added impetus, and everything that could go wrong has done so. In June 1987 the England selectors sent out forty letters to players enquiring about their availability for the World Cup in India and Pakistan later that year. Now, I've no idea if my name was the twentieth or the fortieth on their list, but I was thrilled to get one of those letters. There were ten days between the letters being sent and the squad being announced, and in that time Hampshire had to play a strong Essex side on a green wicket at Portsmouth, which was about the last thing I needed. I made three 0s - c East b Lever each time. Two of the dismissals were tame leg side catches, and for the other I got a ball that nipped back a long way. A couple of plays and misses and a dropped catch would have worked wonders, but it didn't work out that way, and I wasn't picked for the tour.

Everyone gets unlucky breaks in their careers - David Gower

and Jack Russell come instantly to mind, and I don't think my brother had a fair crack at Test level. People always said that he had a weakness facing short-pitched bowling, but if he wasn't as partial to it as me, he still scored a great many runs against it, and there were few better players of spin in the country. He was given his chance before he was at his best, and ignored when he was. He wouldn't want me to make any excuses on his behalf, but I know that he was a bit disenchanted with Test cricket by the time he retired.

Personally speaking, I don't feel I have any reason to grumble. I was only 18 when I played my first county championship game for Hampshire against Lancashire in 1983. I was delighted to make a century on my debut, because it's the sort of thing that everyone dreams about, but I've always had this sneaking suspicion that it owed as much to Jack Simmons as to my own efforts. My brother had already scored a hundred in the match, and as we got to the last over of the day I was 89 not out. We were playing on a wicket that was sited on side of the square, and for the last over, which was to be bowled by Jack, the short boundary was on the leg side. Jack was an experienced enough bowler not to bowl anything loose on the leg stump, and as it was obvious that we would declare at our overnight position, I had no great expectations of reaching my maiden hundred. Jack fired in the first ball outside the off stump and I tried to hit it too hard and missed. Off the next four deliveries I managed to scramble five runs, and found myself on strike to the last ball of the day needing six to complete my century. What did Jack bowl? A slow full toss on leg stump which I could smack out of the park for 6. Jack has never admitted he did it deliberately; he's such a lovely man that he wouldn't want me to think I'd been handed my century on a plate, but he's not a bad enough bowler to bowl a slow full toss at that stage of the game, and I will be eternally grateful to him for it.

That hundred certainly meant that I never had to go through any anxiety wondering if and when my first century for the county would ever come, and gave me the confidence to score two more in my brief run in the first team while Gordon Greenidge and Malcolm Marshall were away with the West Indies World Cup squad. I was quite lucky as well with the third century that I made in the game against Gloucestershire. I was dropped off a caught and bowled chance when I was on 0 by John Childs, and for the rest of the innings he and David Graveney bowled unchanged.

It's often not a question of how many runs you get, but in what situation, and with who watching, that can determine whether you get picked for the national side, and I have often scored my runs at the right time and the right place. This obviously isn't all down to luck, but there have been times when I've thanked my stars that I haven't received the unplayable ball. I played one crucial match-winning innings in the Benson & Hedges quarter-final against Worcestershire in 1988 when I made an unbeaten 87. The pitch was green and spiteful and in a low scoring game Nigel Cowley and I guided Hampshire home with three wickets to spare. That was a wicket on which the ball was moving all over the place, and whilst I played well, anyone would have needed a degree of good fortune to last as long as I did. That knock did my England prospects no harm; Micky Stewart was at the game, and I think it was that innings, together with my cameo in the final, that persuaded him to pick me for the 4th Test against the West Indies later that season.

I've also been lucky with injuries – mine and other people's. I've only missed two Tests through injury and both times I was fit enough to be selected for the one after. The first time I got injured in a Test I felt it was the end of the world. Halfway through my innings of 96 against the Australians at Lord's in 1989 I pulled a hamstring, but I just carried on batting regardless. Within a few days I knew it wasn't going to recover for Edgbaston, and I went off to a pub by myself to have a good moan about my luck. For the first time I felt as if I had scored enough runs to be sure of making the next Test, and after all the hard work and worry the chance was going to be taken away from me. I think I've got a slightly better perspective on it now though!

The one time I was undeniably lucky with injuries was just before the Headingley Test against the Australians in the same year. I was feeling fairly miserable having received David Gower's phone call telling me that I hadn't made the side, but after a brief break to get over the disappointment, it was business as usual with a Sunday League game against Middlesex. During the course of this match David Turner nicked a ball to Mike Gatting who split his finger and had to withdraw from the England squad. I felt rotten for Gatt, but I couldn't help thinking: 'God's smiling on me', as I was sure that I was bound to be called up in his place. I couldn't believe it when Kim Barnett was chosen ahead of me. The next thing I heard was that Steve Barwick had bounced Ian Botham and had hit him in the face, so that he too had to step down. This time I was chosen, and to my mind justice was done. I went to Headingley with something to prove; although we lost the game I was pleased with my 66 on a treacherous pitch, and that innings marked the beginning of a good run against the tourists that summer.

Luck can come in all sorts of subtle ways that have nothing to do with selection, dismissals, or injuries, but are just as influential to the way one feels about oneself and the game. I have talked about my bad patch last summer, and although I had turned the corner by the time we played the Benson & Hedges final against Kent, I was still somewhat unsure of myself. It was overcast and the ball was swinging when I went out to bat, and because they knew that I hadn't been in the best of nick, they decided to put me under pressure by setting attacking fields. This turned out to be just what I needed. It meant that I got full value for my shots from the start, and in next to no time I had 20 on the board and my confidence back.

This was exactly the right tactic for the Kent captain to adopt; it just didn't work out as he had planned. Angus Fraser was in tears at the end of a one-day international in Jamaica because he had been hit for 14 runs in his final over. I told him that he hadn't bowled badly; it was the batsman who had taken a few risks because he

had to, and had got lucky. Getting hit was no reflection on Angus'
skill as a bowler. Nine times out of ten the batsman would have
got out attempting those kinds of shots against a mainline bowler,
but this was the time he got away with it.

It would be wrong to say that I never get flustered about
playing and missing, but it certainly bothers me less than it used to.
In the second innings of the Barbados Test in 1990 I was dropped
four times on my way to scoring 62, but I never felt as if I was
playing badly. It was one of those innings when I didn't play and
miss, but whenever I did play a false stroke the ball took the
outside edge. Every batsman plays and misses and there's no point
giving it too much thought. It's as integral a part of the game as
the weather. We were unlucky that so much rain fell in Trinidad
on the same tour when we were so close to going into an
unbeatable two Test lead, but it's happened in the past when it's
been to England's advantage. I certainly don't blame the West
Indians for slowing down their over rate to force the draw. We
would have done exactly the same if the positions had been
reversed, and besides the bowlers' run ups were so damp that the
game should probably never have been restarted.

You can spot some pieces of bad luck coming from a long way
off. I'd made 58 in the first innings of the last Test in Perth on the
1990-1 tour, and I was going well in the second with a high
percentage of my runs coming in boundaries. It was the first match
that I had felt in good form, and I was confident of making a
decent score. Alec Stewart went half-forward twice to Terry
Alderman in the same over, and on both occasions the ball nipped
back and rapped him on the pads. The umpire gave both not out
though from where I was standing at the non-striker's end they
looked well worth a shout. After the second appeal was turned
down Terry Alderman went berserk with the umpire, shouting all
sorts of abuse. I knew that the umpire was feeling the pressure, so I
said to myself: 'Don't get hit on the pad when you're at the other
end, whatever you do, because he's bound to give the next one
out.' Sure enough, in the very next over from Alderman I got hit

145

on the pad by a ball that the TV replay showed wasn't going to hit another set of stumps, and I was on my way back to the pavilion. That dismissal just about summed up my whole series.

If I was in any doubt that the Australian tour was ill-starred as far as I was concerned, I had it rubbed in when I got back to England. I'd organised a cab to collect me from Heathrow, so that I could get back to Kath and Harrison as soon as possible, and I was sent the only taxi driver stupid enough to park on a double yellow line outside the arrival terminals. All my mates were safely on their way home while I was left standing around, freezing to death in a thin England blazer and a short-sleeved shirt, for an hour and three-quarters, waiting for the driver to retrieve his cab from the police car pound. I suppose the message is: 'When your luck's out, your luck's out', and there's nothing you can do but have a laugh about it later.

CHAPTER EIGHT

SUPPORT

Nobody operates in isolation, and cricketers are no exception. When Robin scores a Test century at Lord's it's tempting to imagine that the success is his alone, and to forget the network of family, friends, and colleagues who provide him with the structure and support to give of his best. A cricketer needs talent, mental strength, and single-mindedness to reach the top, but he also needs people that he can trust and talk to when he is feeling down and who will smooth over the day to day minutiae of life for which he has no time. As Neil Fairbrother says: 'I play my best cricket when I feel comfortable in my surroundings. Problems like worrying about the mortgage or one's place in the side are bound to crop up from time to time, and I need people around me whom I can trust to talk to about them.' Looking at the fate of those English footballers who signed for foreign clubs and let the lure of the lira make them neglect their emotional life one can see the truth in this. It is only players like Kevin Keegan and Gary Lineker who bothered to learn the language and tried to make new friends who made a success of their careers abroad.

Cricketers spend so much of their time away from home that the team becomes almost a substitute family. In this context, it is probably more important for cricketers to get along with each other than for most other team sport participants. Relationships between team mates can become confused when two players are vying for the same place, but the lasting nature of many friendships is proof that there is plenty of enjoyment and support to be found amongst colleagues.

Feeling valued by the club is altogether more tricky. No matter what a club does to help, most players won't feel valued until they can command a regular place in the side. Neil Fairbrother had been in and out of the England set-up for some years, but it was

147

only on the World Cup tour to Australia and New Zealand that he finally felt part of the squad. Talking about the problem helps, but even so, Brian Mason says that many players still feel that it is a sign of weakness to open up to one another. 'Whenever I work with a player I start by asking if he has any problems or worries I should know about. More often than not there will be something on his mind that doesn't necessarily have anything to do with cricket which he hasn't dared tell anybody else and is affecting his game.'

Cricket teams exist to play cricket and not to provide a forum for dealing with players' personal problems, and as such it's reasonable to expect the players to know how to look after themselves and get along with one another. Yet a benevolent, paternalistic attitude from the team management and senior pros towards the younger players can have a profound effect on their performance. Brian Mason feels that much of Graeme Hick's early problems at Test level had as much to do with fitting in to the side as with any technical deficiencies. Hick is a quiet, reserved man who comes from a sheltered upbringing in Zimbabwe. On coming to this country he joined Worcestershire, a smallish county with a family-like set-up; he fitted in immediately and scored thousands of runs for them. He didn't know any of the England players particularly well when he was selected for the national side, and what with the extra pressure of media attention, he felt like a fish out of water.

Every club will make some efforts to make new players feel welcome. The England team has a tradition of sitting newcomers next to the captain or chairman of the selectors at the pre-Test dinner, and someone always makes a point of mentioning them in a speech. Mike Brearley remembers Tony Greig and John Edrich being particularly reassuring and helpful in calming his nerves. Some players have little difficulty adjusting to making the step up to Test cricket, and David Gower was one such person. 'I took it that I had a job to do and I was just happy to be in the side. I suppose that it might have been different if I had been making my debut against the West Indies. As it was we were playing a sub-standard Pakistan side against whom I had already scored a hundred in a one-day international, and I felt as if I was on the crest of a wave.'

Other players find the transition less easy. They may be just as talented but are lacking in self-confidence. Chris Smith never found being part of an unfamiliar team much of a problem, but he believes that Robin blossoms when he is amongst team mates whom he knows and who know him. 'As a newcomer he was probably more inhibited than he would have liked. He needs to be boisterous and rowdy in the dressing-room, because he's not naturally self-confident. He tries to create an air of exuberance which he hopes will infiltrate his batting. It's important that team mates allow him the freedom to do this, and he's fortunate to be in sides where he now gets it.'

Senior players whose places are well established within the team can lose their way too. Professional cricket is a stressful business, and, as no one will need reminding after last winter's trip to India and Sri Lanka, it doesn't get much more stressful than touring. Various reasons have been put forward for England's failure in the sub-continent, from poor team selection, through bizarre itinerary and lack of preparation on turning wickets, to simply not being good enough. The relative merits of each argument are immaterial to this discussion, but what is of relevance is that problems such as these, that might have been coped with quite easily at home, take on another dimension abroad.

Niggles and irritations are par for the course on any tour. To a certain extent players have to, and always have had to, adapt to survive, but things can be made easier or more difficult for them. It would obviously be an advantage if players went on tour enthusiastically looking forward to new cultural experiences, but such are the demands of international sport today that most will be thinking of nothing but the cricket. Just as one doubts that many Olympians gave much thought to Gaudi's buildings in Barcelona, it is unrealistic to expect professional cricketers to have much interest in Moghul architecture. Even as cultured and resourceful a player as Mike Brearley struggled on his first tour to South Africa. 'It wasn't that I was homesick, because I didn't have any close family with whom I was living at the time. I was just immature. I wasn't playing well, and through not practising properly I began to play worse. I grew frustrated at not getting into the Test side, and then felt bored and apart from the team for the rest of the tour.'

The success of a tour is judged by how many cricket matches are won, and everything should be geared to providing not just the right physical but also the right psychological environment to achieve it. If this leads to accusations of being blinkered, then so be it. There are no easy overseas tours any more; standards have risen in countries that were traditionally regarded as weak, schedules that could once accommodate the odd tiger shoot are now tightly packed and the players need all the help they can get.

Many of the Test playing countries who tour England have incalculable advantages. There are the obvious ones such as the smaller distances between venues, a programme that allows four or five first-class games before the first Test with at least one between each Test, and many of the players have previously represented counties or league teams. But there are other advantages which, if less important, are significant nonetheless. As a result of playing in England, and because this country has sizeable West Indian, Indian, and Pakistani communities, many visiting players have family and friends over here who provide a ready-made home environment in which to step. Manifestly, these advantages cannot be reproduced when England go on tour, but in their absence players should be given as long as possible to acclimatize in a new country. The idea of an England A tour to allow young players the opportunity to play in different countries was a step in the right direction, but its effect has been somewhat nullified by the small number who have graduated to the full team.

None of this can guarantee success, but it can make it more likely. Most English players look forward most of all to a tour of Australia, not just because it's the Ashes that are at stake, but because the country has a recognizably similar culture – arguably with one or two improvements. With such expectations of enjoyment, there must be a better chance of doing well. Of course, even a tour to Australia can go disastrously wrong for all sorts of reasons, as England found to their cost in 1990-1, but this only serves to illustrate how difficult it can be to balance the needs of sixteen players whose usual systems of support are for the most part denied to them for three months.

Just how problematic touring can be is apparent from Robin's Test record at home and abroad. Seven of his Test centuries have come in this country, and only one, in the final Test of the last tour, overseas. Doubtless, unfamiliarity with local conditions have contributed to this, but in view of the fact that his best performances overseas have coincided with or come just after a visit from close family, it would be foolish to ignore this influence.

Robin is unusual, not so much because he comes from a tightly-knit family, though that is something of a rarity in itself these days, but because up until the beginning of the 1992 season he had played most of his first-class cricket with his brother. Such proximity might have driven some brothers apart, but it brought Chris and Robin even closer together. 'Things did get claustrophobic at times,' says Chris, 'but when either of us got touchy, the other would intuitively know when to back off. Our closeness is borne of mutual respect. I think he's a kind, sensitive man, who has become a very fine cricketer. If I hadn't received the job offer from Perth I could easily imagine myself thoroughly enjoying playing county cricket alongside him for the next five to ten years.'

Both Chris and Robin drew great pleasure from their close relationship, but having an elder brother who knew him and his game inside out was not without its drawbacks for Robin, as Chris explains. 'For years and years, whenever things were going wrong with his game, either in the nets or in the middle, I would be the one to mention it to him. Many was the time when he would join me at the wicket and play like a complete idiot for a couple of overs, but after a quiet word from me he would settle down and time the ball beautifully. Very rarely would he come to me and say that something was wrong, because even from the earliest days in the nets at home in South Africa I would be the one to tell him that last week he was playing in one way and this week it was different. The result was that he was always in good technique and he never had to work it out for himself.'

None of this was a particular problem until Robin went on tour with people who didn't know him well. Chris Smith continues: 'Robin is either playing extremely well or very badly; there's little in between. He makes a few low scores, loses confidence, puts himself under greater pressure, and the wheels fall off. What he then needs is someone who knows his game inside out, and who knows how to talk to him in the right way to reassemble the pieces. When I met up with him at nets before the third Test in Sydney in January 1991, I was amazed to find that everything that can go wrong with Robin's technique when he is out of form had done so. It was clear Bruce Reid had got on top of him - his head was pointing towards cover, he was trying to play balls on middle stump down to fine leg, and his front leg wasn't getting forward. As a result the ball was appearing to move prodigiously in the air, which it wouldn't if his head was straight, he was hitting balls that should have gone through mid-on behind square, and yet no one had said anything to him about it. Robin always bats on leg stump, but this was playing into Bruce Reid's hands. It meant that all corridor of uncertainty balls were on off stump, and there was little margin for error. I suggested that he bat on middle or middle and off and muddle up Bruce Reid's angles. The corridor of uncertainty balls could then be left alone, and if he bowled at the stumps Robin could hit him back through mid-on. He adopted this method in Sydney and looked better in the first innings than he had done previously. He got a little not out in the second, and his tour improved from then on. The point is that given Robin is not the best analyzer of his own game, why didn't someone point this out to him? Having someone to organize the practice is all very well, but maybe a coach who knew each player's game intimately and knew what words to use to get the best results would be more helpful.

'Robin's a quiet, unassuming man when he's not with the lads, and he does need the support of the family to feel secure. Obviously I like having my family around me too, but he needs them far more than I do. I predicted that 1992 was going to be a difficult year for Robin long before the season started, not because I thought that the Pakistani bowlers would test him any more than any others, but for the same reasons that he had always found touring a struggle. He would have the advantage of being at home with Kathy and Harrison, but for the first time he wouldn't have me to talk to about his cricket. When you put that against a good Pakistani bowling side I'm not surprised that he found 1992 a tricky season. It may have been good for him in the long run because he was forced to talk to other people whom he wouldn't normally have approached, and in the end by all accounts he had mastered Mushtaq Ahmed.'

Test match cricket is a year round occupation, and a married player needs a wife with the qualities of a latter day saint. She must be able to look after the nuts and bolts of running a home at the same time as providing reassurance when it's needed. Robin is fortunate to have Kathy. 'It sometimes feels as if Robin's world is the size of a cricket ball,' says Kathy. 'His mind is so channelled on cricket that he doesn't want to know about mundane family matters; at home, he just asks me to tell him what he's doing. His moods are usually determined by how well he's playing. If things are going badly he'll get depressed and introverted, and he won't be interested in anything else until the problem is sorted. Any spare time is spent in practice, even though sometimes I think he goes over the top, and would be better off forgetting about things for a while.

'I try not to let his moods affect mine, but invariably I do feel low if he gets a run of under 10s because I know what he will be like when he gets home. I try my best to cheer him up, but it's hit

153

and miss whether it works. When Robin first went on tour a lot of people warned me not to tell him about anything that might be going wrong at home, but I decided that honesty was the best policy. On one tour our old house in Romsey came close to being washed away in a flood, and I was up every two hours checking the water level. I didn't hide that from him but neither did I exaggerate it to make him feel guilty for being away. I know that he can't fly home, and I wouldn't expect him too even if he could; I just like him to know what's going on, and I think he appreciates it that way too.

'Robin's a big softy at heart. He hates disappointing people, and often accepts so many cricketing social engagements that we have no time to spend as a family or with our close friends. I know that this is part of the job, but it was getting out of hand. Recently I decided enough was enough and that he could go to some of them without me. It's not that Robin doesn't value the time he spends with me and Harrison, he just finds it hard to say no. He always seems to play better when we join him on tour, and when he does get a low score he prefers spending a quiet night in his room with us to going out and having a beer with the lads. Robin's not a very worldly person, and he feels safest at home. It's only there that he can truly express himself. Often he'll come home and have a good moan about someone, and I'll tell him to say what he's just said to me to the person concerned, but he won't do it. He's just the same in the car; if someone cuts him up he'll be swearing under his breath, but he'll never beep the horn to let the other driver know how he feels.'

Everyone needs support, and professional sportsmen in the public eye need it more than most, though what form that support will take depends on the individual. Some will be more self-contained than others, but players and coaches ignore the importance of outside support to their cost. The last word on the subject should go to David Gower. 'If there's no reservoir to draw strength from, no bank to tap into, you're in trouble. It can be a sympathetic ear from a good friend, a kind word from a colleague, or whatever. Cricket doesn't have to be a solo effort. What Brian Mason has proved to me is that having someone who you trust, who shows faith in you and gives you confidence, is more valuable than virtually anything else.'

ROBIN'S STORY

I'm the first to admit that I need help, and I couldn't begin to thank my parents, Kathy, Chris, coaches and friends for the support they have given me over the years. Cricket is a psychological game and when you lose your way, which everyone does from time to time, you need people around who know what makes you and your game tick, and who can get you back on track. I've been extremely lucky to have parents who have been prepared to spend time and money encouraging me, an elder brother to guide me, and a wife who puts up with the lifestyle of a professional cricketer.

I wanted to get the thanks in early on, because like many of us, I can easily take my family and friends for granted. This certainly happened last year, when I ended up being really nice to everyone except those whom I really care about. I've always hated the thought of someone saying, 'Robin Smith's an unpleasant bloke', and so I've tended to over-compensate for this by accepting every invitation that's come my way. It worked against me last November when I agreed to attend a dinner on the same day as the England v South Africa rugby match for which I had been offered tickets. I don't plan to abandon going to formal engagements because it's part of the job, but I am going to be more strong-minded about which I accept, and if some people take offence that's just too bad. I'm not particularly confident among strangers so it's ridiculous to spend all my free time in situations where I can't relax. Besides how can I be a good husband, father, son, and friend, if I don't spend any time with the people who matter to me?

My Mum and Dad have always been on hand to give me advice or a shoulder to cry on although when I first came to this country it was Chris whom I primarily relied upon. He was instrumental in my coming to Hampshire, and he eased my introduction into the ways of county cricket and English life. I was never given a hard time by anyone at the club for being Chris' younger brother, and the only pressure on me was Chris singing my praises about how I was a better player than him. I suppose some people might have found it hard to live up to such high expectations, but I enjoyed the feeling of being kept on my toes and it was fantastic to have someone openly affirming their belief in my talent.

Chris was a big help in all sorts of ways. He helped me to think about my batting, and was always ready with new ideas and information to improve it. In the middle he knew exactly the right way to talk to me if I was too confident or too humble, and he understood my style. He was adept at taking quick singles which was just what I like as I need a fair amount of the strike to get my rhythm and continuity going. Most of all though, I appreciated his companionship; we spent a lot of our lives travelling, practising, and playing together and I miss his sense of humour. It was especially good fun playing alongside him in the last two years of his career, when, to say the least, he was less agile in the field. Seeing the pain on his face when the captain announced that we'd lost the toss and that we were fielding brought much pleasure to a hard day's work.

It may seem odd to call a home season in which I averaged 45 in Tests and picked up three Man of the Match awards in the Texaco games disappointing, but 1992 fell below my high standards. I would have had a hard time against Mushtaq's leg spin even if Chris had been around, but the fact that he had left Hampshire to work in Australia undoubtedly made things worse. I'd got used to talking to him in a certain kind of way and to him telling me where I was going wrong. As it was, there was a slight void period when I was struggling to get to grips with my game and no one was coming to me and I wasn't going to anyone for help.

It took time for me to adapt and get support elsewhere, and the person who came to my rescue was our Hampshire coach, Tim Tremlett. Tim had been a successful county player in the early eighties, and had always taken a keen interest in me and was a good analyst of my game. Like everyone else, Tim was reluctant to step forward with advice at first. Maybe he didn't want to look as if he was trying to take over from Chris, because he knew no one could replace him. In any case it's always a little difficult approaching someone who you regard as a better batsman to tell him what he's doing wrong. When Tim and I did start working together I found his advice extremely helpful.

It's when you start thinking you know it all that you get problems, and that's why it's so important to have a coach and mentor who knows you as well off the cricket field as on it. Whenever Graham Gooch has a problem, he goes straight to Keith Fletcher or Geoff Boycott. Odd as it may seem, it's just as vital to talk to people and get your game videoed and analyzed when you are playing well because then you've got people who know what your technique should look like, and who can suggest refinements in a relaxed atmosphere. I like to think that I am a big enough person to listen to whatever anyone has to say. I believe that most people only have my best interests at heart and that I can sift out what I find useful, but when you are playing badly you only want to listen to someone who you really trust. Tim now knows my moods and personality and I will be looking to him more than anyone else for guidance in the future.

The county has always looked after me, and I can see myself playing out the rest of my career for Hampshire. I have close friends at the club whom I'll talk to about personal matters, and though I'm friendly enough with everyone else you can't become good mates with everybody. I go out of my way not to get on the wrong side of people. I'm not a great one for sticking my neck out, or arguing with someone if I think he's in the wrong, and I tend to keep quiet and let any chance remarks go over my head. My view is that we're at the club to do well for the county, each other, and ourselves, and we shouldn't let anything get in the way of that. As I've said before, cricket is a tough game; the club's needs come first and it chooses the players who it thinks will achieve the best results. It can be very sad when a close friend is dropped from the side, or worse still released by the county, but you have to try and see the positive side of room being made for younger players. When Allan Lamb was out caught behind in the last of the one-day internationals against Pakistan, I felt emptier than I ever had before, because I knew it was the last time I was going to bat with him for England. I would have loved him to go out with a decent score, but it wasn't to be. Yet the middle of my innings wasn't the time to get sentimental; there was plenty of time for that later. I had to re-focus my concentration and get on with the business of winning the match.

I didn't have any great expectations of being made welcome when I was first selected for England, because I thought that the others would regard me as something of an impostor, having been born and bred in South Africa. I hadn't come up through the ranks of schoolboy cricket, and after a four year qualifying period I was given the opportunity to play for my adopted country. For this reason, David Gower will always be special to me. David was playing his 100th Test, and had just walked into the dressing-room having got out to a lazy shot for which he knew he was going to be crucified in the press the next day. Ambrose was steaming in from the sightscreen, and I was getting more and more nervous waiting for my turn to bat. Barely had David taken off his pads when he tapped me on the shoulder and said: 'Do you like chatting before going out to bat?' I couldn't believe that someone I had always looked up to could be so thoughtful towards me; I nodded, and he sat down. We passed the time in idle conversation, and we've been good friends ever since.

Allan Lamb is another person who I've felt has been behind me ever since I started playing for England, and over the last four years he's become my biggest mate. Lamby has been unbelievably kind, and his positive attitude has certainly rubbed off on me. People have said that he's a bad influence. I know that he can be fairly forthright and that he's not on the best of terms with everyone, but he did everything he could to make me feel part of the side from the word go. I think he understood the problems I might have about my nationality, and he was determined to give me the benefit of as much of his experience as possible. It was Lamby who showed me the ropes, by telling me how things worked behind the scenes. He taught me things like which officials to talk to, and which reporters were friendly and which ones hostile.

I also believe that I owe a special debt of gratitude to Lamby for my appearance at Lord's against the Australians in 1989. I'd been delighted at being picked for the squad having originally been left out of the side that played at Headingley, but it didn't take much to realize that I wasn't going to make the final team. Allan had a slight injury, but nothing would normally make him miss a Test at Lord's on a flat wicket. He's a tough character, and yet even before he had a fitness test, he came up to me and said: 'Have a good net this morning and get your mind right, because I don't think I'll be playing.' His place was pretty much secure in the side after his century in the first Test, and I think he decided that as he wasn't 100% fit he would give me the chance.

Despite David and Allan's support my first few Tests were characterized by a distinct absence of team spirit. There was no continuity in the side; the selectors seemed to have no faith in the teams they chose, and the players had no faith in the selectors. It wasn't even as if the players could help each other too much, because everyone was far too preoccupied with keeping their own place in the side to have too much time for anyone else. I've always found that I play my best cricket when I'm in a team with players whom I know well. Although people have come and gone since Graham Gooch took the England side to the West Indies in 1990, there has been nothing like the wholesale changes of my first eight Tests, and I have felt much more a part of the team as a result. Even so, playing for England does throw up some oddities. I saw this bloke wandering around in an England T-shirt in the hotel lobby in Trindad, and I turned to one of the other players and said: 'Who the hell is that?' I'd never set eyes on Chris Lewis before he joined the team in the Caribbean.

You can't do everything for a newcomer because he has to learn to look after himself, but I've tried hard to give young players confidence, and to make them feel valuable members of the side. Graeme Hick didn't have the easiest introduction to the England set-up; the media interest was intense, and it always seemed as if the opposition bowlers tried that little bit harder when he arrived at the wicket. I became very fond of Hicky over this time and went out of my way to gee him up or commiserate with him when I thought he wanted it. The Texaco game against Pakistan at the Oval last year was one of the first occasions when I spent any length of time with him at the wicket. I had been dismissed cheaply, and I was running for Neil Fairbrother. Hicky looked shell-shocked after his first eight deliveries, and I said to him: 'Everybody in this ground knows what a great player you are; just relax and show them', which he did. Again, I was more excited than he was when he hit Mushtaq almost out of the ground at Old Trafford later that season, and no one was more delighted than me when he proved his worth in India last winter.

Looking at my career it's obvious that I haven't done exceptionally well on tour. Some people have written that it's because I have problems adjusting to overseas conditions, but apart from those in India, I don't think the wickets are that different. Sure, some of them are a little bouncier and more uneven than English surfaces, but they are quite nice to bat on, so I don't feel that is the whole reason by any means. My batting relies heavily on continuity, and on tour I don't get that many knocks between Test matches. Everything happens so fast that there isn't time to take stock with friends and family and think about what is going right or wrong. It's not that I want to be anti-social because I enjoy a drink and a laugh as much as anyone, it's just that I need a bit of peace and quiet as well. With that in mind I don't think it's surprising that I've tended to play my best cricket when my family is around.

The 1990/1 Australian tour was particularly difficult for me, as Kath was about 8 months pregnant with Harrison when I left, and I was understandably concerned about her. I like to think that I am sufficiently professional not to let such domestic concerns affect my form, but if I am honest I think that it did in the early part of the tour. It wasn't that I was consciously thinking about Kath as I went out to bat, but I would be hard pushed to say that I gave my preparation the usual 100% effort and concentration. After one innings in which I was out to a poor shot Geoff Boycott wrote: 'What else do you expect when he's thinking about a baby at home? Robin Smith should sharpen up his ideas. Millions of people have had babies all over the world in the last few thousand years.' I agree that I shouldn't have played the shot, but I would also say: 'What does Geoff Boycott know about what it's like to have a baby when he's got no family of his own?'

What made things worse was that I wasn't able to fly home to see Kath as I had hoped. I knew there was never any chance of being at home for the birth in early December, but I was optimistic about missing the state game against Victoria before Christmas and nipping back to England for a couple of days. I had mentioned this to Graham Gooch and Micky Stewart before the tour started. They had no objections in principle, though they offered no guarantees, and I went ahead and organized a return first-class flight courtesy of the *Sunday Mirror*. Shortly after the first Test it was obvious that I wasn't going to be allowed to go home; the team was playing badly, we had injury problems, and my own form was poor. I was in a terrible state because I knew how much Kathy was looking forward to seeing me, and I didn't want to let her down because she was in a highly emotional state after the birth. Rightly or wrongly, I decided to delay telling her the bad news till the last moment. We used to speak every night on the phone, and it reached the point where I dreaded calling her

161

because it was heartbreaking having to lie. As you can imagine she wasn't too impressed when I broke the news; she understood that there was nothing I could do about it, but to this day I don't think she believes that I was ever really going to come home. The best compromise that we could manage was that she and Harrison join us on tour earlier than planned for the third Test in Sydney, and whether it was coincidence or not, my results improved on their arrival.

One thing I've learnt from this is that if we have a second child we'll plan it so that I'm in the country for the birth. There's no way that Kathy would go through all that again if I'm not here. We'll just have to pray that we can get the timing right. September or October would be an ideal time, but if we got it wrong I would be prepared to pull out of a Test match if necessary. Next time my family will come first.

The other reason that things perked up in Sydney on that tour was that my brother arrived. He was in charge of a tour that had flown in to watch the Test, and the time he spent working in the nets and chatting with me was invaluable. We worked on my technique, but equally importantly he built up my confidence. He helped to instill in me the belief that I was good enough to delay making a decision about what shot to play until the last possible moment. I stopped lunging at the ball too early, and exploded into my shots instead. Micky Stewart had done his best, but he couldn't offer me the help that my brother could.

Nothing is straightforward in cricket, and you can never say a particular good innings was solely down to a single cause. Maybe my form on that Australian tour would have got better regardless of whether Kathy, Harrison, and Chris had been around. I played better in the West Indies after Kathy arrived, and likewise in India things began to look up for me the day before Kathy joined me in Bombay. On the other hand, she tends to come out towards the end of the tour, by which time I've usually got used to the climate and conditions. What I can say is that I am a family man at heart, and given the choice of having them with me or leaving them

162

behind, I would have them with me. Some players seem to need less support than others, but I'm not ashamed to admit that I need my family and friends a great deal. I've got a family I love and friends I care about; all I need to do is ensure I make the best of them.

CHAPTER NINE

THE TEST MATCH

2nd INNINGS v PAKISTAN. 5th TEST at THE OVAL. AUGUST 1992.

Pakistan were well in command of the match after two days play, and I studied the weather forecast more closely than usual on the Saturday morning. Rain had threatened for a few days, and I was praying for the promised thunderstorms to arrive. Apart from the three occasions when Wasim and Waqar rattled through us at Lord's, Headingley, and the first innings at the Foster's Oval, the series had been fiercely contested. We were all mentally exhausted, and I was rather looking forward to putting my feet up for the day – not exactly the best of attitudes with which to approach the start of play.

The weather was overcast when I arrived at the ground, and though a few of us looked up anxiously, willing the dark clouds to roll in, it was clear that play would start on time. I think that Goochie sensed that some of us didn't have our minds wholly on the job, so before we went out to practise he gave us a schoolmasterly talking to, along the lines of: 'Lets get our minds right and the team back in the game. We've messed things up for a couple of days, so let's fight for our pride and country.' Some of Goochie's enthusiasm rubbed off on me, but even so I was still secretly hoping that my series had ended. It hadn't been the best of summers, but a Test average of around 33 wouldn't have been too dreadful. Goochie had dropped a few broad hints in my direction that I would be going on the India tour regardless of what happened, and I just wanted to put the summer behind me and look forward to the winter.

My foot was still sore from where I had been hit on the toe by one of Waqar's inswinging yorkers in the first innings, which had given him a great deal more amusement than it did me, and the prospect of missing an hour's fielding to have it X-rayed was not entirely unappealing. The X-ray revealed nothing more serious than a bad bruise, and by the time I returned Devon Malcolm had taken a couple of wickets and I began to think more positively about our chances. I knew that the wicket was deteriorating so I reckoned that if we could match their first innings score with our second, they would struggle to win the match. It was disappointing that we couldn't wrap up the tail quickly after those early breakthroughs, but we would probably have settled for a first innings deficit of 173 at the start of the day's play.

During the interval we decided that a safety first policy gave us the best chance of winning the game. Wickets were far more important than runs and our aim was to reach the close with just two wickets down. It was the right plan, but the execution was poor. Alec Stewart was LBW to Waqar for 8, and, if Mike Atherton had been given out the same way to a fair shout next ball, there's no way I would have been barely ready to bat, as I had scarcely put on my pads. Mike didn't survive much longer before edging an outswinger to the keeper, and I found myself walking out to bat at 46-2, a great deal sooner than myself or the team would have liked. There was a lot of talk in the press and on TV about how this second innings was a pressure innings for me, but that's not at all how it felt. It was a crisis innings for England, but not for me. Obviously I wanted to do well, and I realized that a lot depended on at least one batsman staying in and making 150, but going in when the team is so far behind is never the worst time to bat. It's far more nerve-racking when you go in when you're just edging in front and there's a realistic chance of winning. In addition to this, lodged in the back of my mind, was the thought that this was the last time I was going to have to face the Pakistani bowlers in a Test match that summer; even if I didn't do well, there was a nice holiday to contemplate. I was still conscious that I needed 40 to reach my personal goal for the match, but even here the pressure was off slightly; it was going to take much more than that to save the game for England.

I went through my usual routine on the way to the wicket; opening my eyes wide to get used to the light and swinging my bat to warm me up and release tension. I took my usual two leg guard and prepared to face my first ball from Waqar. I took several deep breaths to help me relax and to channel my concentration. I reminded myself to feel light on my feet to give me the confidence to move as late as possible. Waqar gets most of his wickets when batsmen hover on the back foot to full length deliveries, so I looked down the wicket and mentally pushed the bowler's stumps further back; I then imagined Waqar coming in from 30 yards and me moving my feet to the pitch of the ball and seeing it large and clear all the way on to the middle of the bat.

Maybe if I had been less comfortable against short-pitched bowling Waqar would have let go a bouncer first up to remind me what it's all about, but as it was I got the good length inswinger. It wasn't a bad ball; it was touch and go whether I had to play at it, but it was just wide enough for me to shoulder arms. There were cries of 'Well bowled Wicky' from the slips, but I drew a lot of confidence from that ball because I knew that my judgement had been sound. Fielders often say 'Well bowled' as much to put off the batsman as to give the bowler encouragement, but I made it work for me. If that ball was one of Waqar's best, I knew I could handle him.

I got off the mark next ball with a push through mid-wicket for 3; it was a poor shot because the ball was far too straight to work to leg but even so it was nicely timed, and it was good to feel the ball in the middle of the bat so early in the innings. I'm quite superstitious, and as I completed my third run, I made a point of grounding my bat each side of the return crease. I do almost exactly the same thing at the non-striker's end when the bowler is running in, except that then I ground my bat twice each side. I only do it at the start of my innings or for a few overs when a new batsman comes in. I acquired this habit about three years ago, and though I'm not sure exactly how it developed it's designed to bring good luck.

By now my nerves had stopped jangling; I was still tense, but I wasn't quaking in my boots. Mushtaq was brought on straightaway to bowl from the Pavilion end, which again was what I had expected. He had troubled me all summer, had bowled me in the first innings, and it was an obvious ploy. His first ball was too full, and I was able to work it to leg for a couple. The next two were leg breaks, the second of which I missed altogether. I didn't give myself a hard time about this play and miss. Mushtaq deserved the credit for a great delivery, so I forgot about it, and set about refocusing my concentration. I didn't read the next ball at all. Mushtaq had been so accurate throughout the summer that I thought that any ball that far outside the off stump had to be the wrong 'un; it wasn't, but I managed to turn it past the short leg fielder for a single anyway. A lot of the England players, myself included, were surprised at how much turn Mushtaq was able to get. He's the finest spin bowler I've ever faced, and his skill is even more remarkable when one remembers that he's still in his early twenties.

Goochie and I had a brief chat after that over. He isn't in the mould of Allan Lamb as a conversationalist, who relaxes both you and himself by talking about anything but cricket; Goochie's remarks were more on the lines of: 'Keep concentrating; both of us must be here by the close', but they were welcome nonetheless. He's a straightforward man, and it's hard not to be inspired by his determination. I played out the next over from Waqar without scoring, but I was delighted with the way I batted. 90% of Waqar's get out balls are well pitched up, resulting in bowled, caught behind, or LBW decisions, and so one has to look to get forward to him. After three full-length deliveries to which I had done so, Javed brought in a silly mid-off. This was designed to make me more tentative about coming forward, but Waqar's next delivery was a waste. He should have bowled a ball that demanded I play a front foot shot, in the hope that I would be late on it; instead he tried to be too clever and bowled a bouncer, which I could easily duck underneath. By the end of the over I felt that I had got the best of the initial skirmish with Waqar; I hadn't been distracted by the close-in fielder, my defence was solid, and I could sense by the way that Waqar kicked the ball to a fielder that he was getting frustrated.

Goochie then played out a maiden to Mushtaq, which gave me a slight breather. Even so, there was the running between the wickets to think about. The margin of error is sometimes only a few inches in a quick single, and a moment's hesitation or a failure to back up can be fatal. The next over was sure to be the last before tea, and my only goal was to make sure I didn't lose my wicket. Waqar had put another man on the leg boundary indicating that he was going to bounce me. I hardly ever play the hook, so the fielder was there not so much for the catch, but to try and lure me once more into not getting forward. I turned the first ball to leg for a single, and rather hoped that I wouldn't get the strike again before tea. I didn't, though not in the way I had hoped, as Goochie got an edge to the penultimate ball of the session and was caught at second slip. Goochie was furious with himself for getting out at such a critical time, but even so he made time in the tea interval to talk to me about how I might best combat Mushtaq. As I've described earlier in the book, he suggested that I play from the crease, and despite my reservations I decided to follow his advice.

As I walked out after tea my thoughts were centred on being there at the close. I wasn't going to turn down any scoring opportunities, but equally I knew that by playing Mushtaq from the crease I wasn't going to get that many either, and so the bulk of my runs would have to come from loose deliveries from Wasim and Waqar. My cocoon of concentration was disrupted in Mushtaq's first over after tea by some backchat amongst the fielders and I had to pull away as he ran in. Luckily I was in the right frame of mind; I didn't allow myself to get annoyed, I settled down quickly, and punched the next ball through mid-wicket for two.

David Gower was bowled in Waqar's next over. With four

wickets down England were in deep trouble, but I felt as if the pressure on me was lifting. No one in the ground had any great expectations that Mark Ramprakash or I could get England into a winning position, and the Pakistanis must have been hoping that they could wrap the game up that evening. All that was left to play for was some pride, and the outside chance that it would rain for two days solidly.

By now I was beginning to feel more relaxed against Mushtaq. Sometimes you half-heartedly say to yourself 'watch the ball' as the bowler runs in, but now I was saying it and meaning it. As I was no longer worried about going down the wicket to him, I had more time to concentrate on watching which way the ball was spinning out of his hand. I didn't get it right every time, but I certainly improved. Curiously enough, Wasim and Waqar's knack of getting a bright red sheen on one side of the ball worked against Mushtaq, because the contrasting colours of the ball made it easier to pick up the spin.

Waqar was still a real handful; his pace and swing were an awesome proposition, but it was a point of honour for me not to give him the satisfaction of getting me out. After all my problems, I wanted to make certain that it was I who had the last laugh. A couple of overs later I was disappointed to miss out on a four when a square drive went straight to cover, because I sensed that Waqar must be nearing the end of his spell and I felt that a boundary would guarantee he came off. Yet Waqar is nothing if not an attacking bowler; he keeps his fielders up around the bat, and when he fails to swing the ball or is slightly off line he gives the batsman a chance to score. Two out of his next three deliveries were short outside the off stump; the first I cut high over third man, the second in front of square, and with these two boundaries I knew I had achieved my short-term goal of seeing Waqar out of the attack.

Wasim replaced Waqar at the Vauxhall end. I've always had problems against left armers, and they don't come any better than Wasim. The pace and bounce he gets from such a short run up are astonishing. I called for new gloves, partly because the old ones were wet through and partly to give myself time to think about the new bowler. I altered my guard to middle and off, with the idea of giving myself more security outside the off stump and making Wasim bowl more at my body. This tactic made the cut less productive, but I would be able to compensate for that with nudges and deflections on the leg side. Facing Wasim also required a mental readjustment; whereas Waqar's wicket taking ball was the inswinger, the only way Wasim was going to dismiss me was by getting me to fish outside the off stump, and so I had to change my pattern of visualization. I was slow to get it right, and I played and missed at Wasim's second ball. It was a good ball, and I gave Wasim a nod in acknowledgement, but I was annoyed with my loss of concentration. Whatever I said to myself clearly worked as I was much more assured in letting a ball go outside the off stump later in the over.

Ramps was given out caught off the glove in Mushtaq's next over. The TV replay showed that he was unlucky, but poor decisions seldom bother me when I'm at the non-striker's end because I've usually got no idea of whether the batsman is out or not. Ramps' dismissal gave me the opportunity to end a tough series on a high note, and my game plan became just a shade more selfish at this point. Half the side were out, Chris Lewis, who is a wonderful striker of the ball had come in, and I saw even less reason to force the pace than before.

My battle with Wasim was a good contest. In his next over I hit one delightful shot for 2 between the bowler and mid-off which gave me immense pleasure, and two balls later he beat me outside the off stump again. Wasim had fired in two inswingers at my pads, and when he bowled his outswinger wide of the off stump I was furious at being tempted by it. My discipline had let me down, and I banged my bat against my hand in irritation.

Mushtaq must have been frustrated by his next over. First I clubbed him a little uppishly through the covers for 4, I then paddled him to fine leg for a couple, and with the last two balls he beat me twice in a row. I wasn't nearly so bothered about playing and missing at Mushtaq because at last I was reasonably happy with my technique against him. I still had trouble picking him, but I knew that his danger ball was the googly that turned out of Wasim's footmarks. Therefore I had decided that if I was in doubt as to which way the ball was turning I would cover my stumps and play for the wrong 'un. If I guessed wrong and it was the leg break it was far more likely that the ball would miss the bat than take the edge.

It was clear by now that Chris Lewis wasn't going to play his normal swashbuckling innings. His confidence wasn't that high after a run of low scores, and he had decided that watchful defence was his best option. With me not looking to take chances either, the game entered a period of relative calm for the first time since the innings had begun. Wasim tried to shake things up by bowling from round the wicket. I straightened up my stance, and although he beat me with a beauty that swung in and moved away after pitching, I was generally playing him with a fair degree of comfort.

That over proved to be Wasim's final fling in that spell. Waqar came on to relieve him, but now even he was slightly on the defensive, posting a man out on the deep cover boundary. I was slightly irritated by this as it meant that I wouldn't get full value for my shots, but I tried to take it as a sign that the Pakistanis acknowledged I was getting on top of the bowling. I got a thick edge to third man off his first ball and scampered a couple of runs. This showed the benefit of knowing your fielders; if someone like Salim Malik had been at third man I would have never attempted the second run, but with Aqib Javed there it was always on. Three balls later I picked up another 2 with a square cut, but after that Chris and I went runless for a few overs. You can't afford to lose concentration when you're up against bowlers of the quality of Mushtaq, Waqar, and Wasim, but it's easy to do in periods of relative quiet and that's just what happened in Waqar's next over. The ball was of a goodish length outside the off stump, and I had a complete brainstorm; I tried to hit it off the back foot on the up through mid on. Luckily it went along the ground, but again I had to force myself to re-focus my concentration. The next delivery was a bouncer which got my adrenalin going again and bolstered my confidence. I've always enjoyed it when the ball is flying around my head, and I ducked this one with ease.

Chris and I had now settled into a pattern. I was taking the quick bowlers and he was taking Mushtaq. It wasn't something we had consciously pre-planned, but both of us were quite happy with the way things were going. If Chris had been given a choice I'm sure he would have opted to face Mushtaq, whilst I am always happiest against pace. Waqar obviously decided that enough was enough and that he wanted to bowl at Chris. At the beginning of his next over he pushed all his fielders back, thereby offering me the single. Chris is no rabbit with the bat, and with only half an hour to go till stumps, I was quite happy to take any runs Waqar was offering, and duly pushed his first ball to deep mid off. When there is so little time to go, I become more aware of the scoreboard than usual, and I put a mental tick against every over that was successfully negotiated.

Chris's athleticism took me by surprise in Waqar's next over. I had clipped an inswinging full toss through mid-wicket and was quite contentedly ambling through for three, when I heard Chris call me back for the fourth. This shows how focused I was on survival; in normal circumstances I would have been on the lookout for any available run to reach my 50 before the end of the day. I was still playing reasonably positively, though, and in the following over I smashed Mushtaq straight for four. I intended to hit it through the covers but I misread the turn, and the ball went back past Mushtaq at catchable height. Technically it was a chance, but the ball was hit so hard that I would have considered myself extremely unlucky if he had caught it.

I was getting quite tired now, and when Aqib came on for the last few overs from the Vauxhall end I had to make myself concentrate harder than ever. I didn't want to let any over-confidence creep in now that the two best fast bowlers were off, and I continued my routine reminders about getting forward. My fifty came up in this over with a cut behind square, and I gave thanks to the Good Lord for it as usual. I was relieved and delighted to reach this personal milestone, just as I had been when I had reached 40 to bring my aggregate for the game to 70, but I was more than aware that the job was only half done.

Javed Miandad tried everything he could in the last few overs to disrupt us and force us into making errors. He brought fielders in close both sides of the wicket to get me to play more off the back foot. He even gave Aamir Sohail one over from the Pavilion end. Sohail presented me with an interesting dilemma. Normally I would have been looking to use my feet against a slow left-armer of his ability. I hate the idea of letting a bowler dictate to me, and if you're prepared to go down the wicket he's never too sure what length to bowl. However, my plan of playing from the crease had proved so effective that I maintained it with Sohail. In the event my decision didn't cost me any runs. Quite apart from not having Mushtaq's turn or variation, he doesn't have his accuracy, and I took six from the over without taking risks. Those were my last aggressive strokes for the day; I shut up shop for the last three overs, and it was a great feeling to walk off undefeated when Dickie Bird called time.

That evening I had a quiet dinner with Kath and a couple of old friends from Southampton who I hadn't seen for a while, and went to bed fairly early. We were badly let down by the weathermen again on the Sunday; we had been promised rain, and the clouds were higher than at any other time in the match. I get anxious much earlier than usual when I know I have to bat at the start of the day's play, so I was a little subdued when I arrived at the ground. I realized that we would probably be beaten but I was determined to enjoy myself anyway. I didn't want to put any extra pressure on myself by getting worked up about the situation, and the only plan that Chris and I made for the day was to try and stick around till lunchtime and see how things looked then.

Re-starting an innings presents certain problems. You've lost the momentum of the previous day, and the fact that you've already got runs on the board can make you relax into over-confidence. I always tell myself that whatever happened yesterday is history, and that I'm starting the day on 0. With this in mind I was content to bide my time from the start and the game remained on a fairly even keel for the first half hour. I forced myself to concentrate hard, picked up the odd single here and there, and let Chris make up his own mind about how to play. Wasim and Waqar opened the bowling, and it was Wasim who gave me the most bother. Waqar seemed to have lost the ability to move the ball away from the bat after his back injury. His inswinger was still lethal, he could make the ball hold its own, and he was very quick, but as long as I could make myself play forward to him I didn't feel in any danger. Wasim was a different proposition. He moved the ball both ways at will, and it was much harder to know which balls to leave. Twice I played at balls that were too close to the off stump to be left only to find the ball move away sharply and beat the bat. There was no point in getting upset; one has to expect the odd unplayable delivery from one of the world's best bowlers.

My first real shot in anger was a pull off Wasim. I rarely play this shot, and it's a sure sign that I was feeling sharp after a good rest the night before. The ball was short outside the off stump; my initial inclination was to cut, but some instinctive voice inside me said: 'What the hell, let's pull.' Not surprisingly with such indecision I mistimed the ball, and instead of going through mid-wicket for 4, it went high over mid-on for 3. I didn't feel it was a risky stroke though; when I attack the ball I attack it hard and with my strength I can be fairly certain that any mishit will clear the infield. Test cricket is all about batsmen and bowlers probing for one another's weaknesses. Wasim clearly thought that he might have spotted one here, because in his next over he gave me another ball to pull, but this time I timed it perfectly through mid-wicket for another 3.

I had always hoped that we could make it through till lunch, but I was just starting to believe that we actually might do it when

Chris played a rash stroke in Mushtaq's next over and was stumped. It was a clever piece of bowling to tuck Chris up, but there was no need for that shot. We had been going along quite comfortably, and I could see the first signs of frustration on the Pakistani faces. There was no reason to change the way I was playing when Derek Pringle came in. I knew that he hadn't been in the best of nick, but he had scored a first-class hundred and there was nothing to be gained by deliberately farming the strike.

Wasim had another go at getting me to pull in his next over, but this time I swayed out the way. I received an unexpected bonus next ball when Waqar presented me with an extra run for an overthrow. It was bad cricket on his part because there was always a comfortable single, and Wasim wouldn't have been best pleased for me to have been given back the strike. I needed to be quick to take the extra run and this was another sign of how much perkier I was feeling compared to the night before.

When Derek Pringle was bowled by Wasim, I realized it was time to start manipulating the strike. I had a quick chat with Neil Mallender when he joined me in the middle. He said that he would much rather take Mushtaq and leave me to face Wasim. This worked well for a few overs; Neil was quite comfortable against the leg-spinner which meant that I could take any runs Mushtaq offered, while at the other end I took as much of the strike as possible. None of the bowlers were giving me problems any more, and I was particularly pleased with a leg glance off Wasim for 4. I had noticed that fine leg had been moved squarer for the mistimed pull, and I played the shot deliberately fine.

Javed Miandad obviously thought that Neil was settling in too well, for when a Wasim bouncer off the last ball of the over prevented me from taking a run, he brought on Waqar to replace Mushtaq. Neil squeezed a single early in the over to give me the strike, and the last four balls of the over provided me with my best moments of the entire series. I'd had such a torrid time in earlier games, and here I was facing my arch rival with every fielder on the fence. It was standard practice, but no strike bowler likes to bowl to such a widespread field, and I couldn't resist a little dig. As I completed my second run from a clip to leg, I said: 'Here you are – the world's best bowler, and not a fielder in sight.' Earlier in the season I had allowed Waqar to get the better of our verbal jousts, but now I was so full of confidence that whatever he said in reply was not going to disturb my concentration. Indeed, maybe it was his rhythm that was disrupted, because no sooner had he brought his field in for the last ball of the over than he bowled a long hop that I could lean back and square cut for 4.

Neil was out early in Wasim's next over, and it was at this point I decided to play for a not out. With only Phil Tufnell and Devon Malcolm to come in there wasn't a hope of winning the game; we were only just level with the Pakistan first innings total and I knew enough about the Cat's and Devon's batting to know that there was no way they were going to survive for more than a few overs. There was nothing for England to salvage from the game so I might as well salvage something for myself, and I made a conscious decision not to play aggressive cricket.

Before he took strike I went to have a quick chat with Phil. This wasn't one of the great tactical discussions of all time. As far as I can remember the conversation went like this: PHIL: Are they fast? ME: You'll be all right. If ever reassurance was futile it was now. He took his customary stride to square leg to his first ball, and was bowled all ends up. Apparently his main concern on returning to the dressing-room was whether it looked bad on the TV replay!

Seeing Devon stride to the wicket brought back memories of a tour match in Trinidad a few years earlier. On that occasion I was on 99, having never scored a century overseas when Devon came into bat. He marched up to me and promised that he would hang around for a while. He promptly took a huge swipe at Patrick Patterson's first ball which went through mid-wicket for 4. I asked him what was going on. He apologised for his rush of blood, and said it wouldn't happen again. He played an immaculate defensive stroke to his second ball, but to his third, the last ball of the over, he had another swipe and was bowled. So this time when I was on 83 and he came up to say that he would look after me while I reached my century, I was under no illusions about the outcome.

I was being offered the single wherever I wanted it, and it was half tempting to take it - to let Devon face the music, and get the innings over and done with, but it wasn't the right way to play the game. I was the senior batsman and I had to take responsibility however hopeless the cause. I was now concentrating as hard as at any other time in the innings, urging myself not to throw my hard work away. I fiddled the strike for a while, but it's an immensely difficult thing to do against top quality bowling. Inevitably there came a time when Devon had to face a full over from Waqar and that was very much that.

I felt like a ton had been lifted from my shoulders when Waqar uprooted Devon's leg stump. A difficult series was over, and I had finished with honour. I remained unbeaten on 84, and it is undoubtedly one of my Test innings of which I am most proud. It's hard to feel as if you are ever truly in against bowlers like Mushtaq, Wasim, and Waqar who are capable of the unplayable delivery at any time, but by the end of the innings I felt that I was on top. I had found an effective way of dealing with Mushtaq, I had more than coped with Wasim and Waqar, and all the problems of the summer dissolved as relief gave way to contentment.

CHAPTER TEN

THE ONE-DAY INTERNATIONAL

5th TEXACO TROPHY GAME. ENGLAND V PAKISTAN. OLD TRAFFORD 1992

This match was a trial of physical stamina and mental endurance as much as anything else. We had played one game in Nottingham on the previous Thursday, another in London on the Saturday that carried over to the Sunday because of bad weather, and here we were in Manchester on the Monday about to start our third Texaco Trophy game in five days. Because these games don't carry the same weight as Test matches, and because some pundits dismiss them as mere crowd pleasers, it's easy to underestimate how hard these games are. The pressure surrounding each game is at least the equal of playing in a one-day county final, and no county side could manage three one-day finals in such a short space of time without suffering from exhaustion.

We had already won the Texaco trophy after the Trent Bridge game, but I had no problem guarding against complacency; there was the thrill of a full house, and besides, I still felt that I had something to prove against the Pakistanis. I was in good spirits at Old Trafford. I had played commandingly at Trent Bridge, my confidence wasn't dented by a low score at Lord's, and I was looking forward to filling my boots with runs to end my international season on a high note.

It's impossible to have a fixed plan for a one-day game, because you can never tell what situation you will face. The only thing I had decided on in advance was a method for playing Mushtaq. After my success in playing him from the crease, I was now sufficiently confident to think about ways of scoring off him. If the ball was on the right length outside the off stump I was going to thrust my left pad toward the ball and sweep. If I connected - fine, and if I didn't the ball would be certain to hit my front leg outside the line of the off stump.

Pakistan batted first and made a more than respectable 254. Graham Gooch and Alec Stewart started our reply at a gallop, and were going along at over 6 an over to reach 98 in the fourteenth over, before Goochie was bowled trying to hit Sohail out of the ground. It may seem an odd admission, but I actually found it difficult going out to bat after such a good start. When the asking rate is 6 an over the pressure is off because you have no choice but to attack from the start of your innings, and if you fail no one will judge you too harshly. Likewise in such a position the fielding side will be quite happy to let you pick up three or four runs an over because you will still be falling behind the run rate, and so they will set their field accordingly. You can have 20 or 30 on the board with little effort in next to no time, and you're then feeling confident enough to step up the pace.

Before I went out to bat at Old Trafford my mind was weighed down with negative possibilities. I knew that the crowd wanted to see me maintain the fluency of the openers, and I was concerned about getting bogged down early on. If I only made, say, 7 off 30 balls, which could easily happen, I would lose the momentum of the innings, and the run rate would creep back up again. It was impossible to believe that Wasim and Waqar could bowl as loosely in their later overs as they had in their first spells, and I also knew that the Pakistanis would now try and close the game down by setting a run saving field. Yet as I walked out to the middle, I tried to replace these negative thoughts with some more positive ones. I reminded myself that England were in the driving seat, that it was my job to be there till the end and that the Pakistanis only had to bowl one bad ball an over for me to accomplish it.

I had a brief verbal interchange with Waqar, which I have described elsewhere, and settled down to face my first ball from Sohail. I had no worries about the wicket, as it was near perfect for batting, so I went through my usual visualization process, reminding myself to keep my weight forward. There was only one ball of the over left, and my intentions were purely defensive; I played the ball quietly and took stock of the situation.

Wasim was brought back into the attack to try to capitalize on Sohail's breakthrough. One criticism that has been levelled against my one-day play is that I fail to look for the quick single, and so I searched the field for gaps. Wasim's stock one-day ball is just short of a length moving into the right hander and there was always the possibility of dropping the ball at my feet, while if he overpitched there were runs to be had square on the off side. Alec was going so well that my immediate plan was to take as many singles as possible, and leave the more aggressive strokeplay to him. As it turned out, Wasim's first ball to me was of a full length on leg stump, and I could easily turn it to square leg to get off the mark.

I took another gentle single in Sohail's next over, and was disappointed to see Stewy give him the charge and get stumped soon after.

With two new batters at the crease there was obviously a danger that Sohail might be able to sneak through his overs without conceding too many runs, but there was no question of my assuming the role of dominant partner and trying to force the pace against him. Neil Fairbrother is one of the best one-day players in the world; if anything, I would have put money on him getting the runs on his home wicket rather than me.

As expected, Wasim was much more menacing in his second spell, and it was not easy to get him away. I tried to cut a ball that was too close to the stumps and was lucky that the edge didn't carry. Later in the same over I had a full-blooded swing at a wide and failed to connect. Oddly enough, I felt much better after that second stroke; the effort expended in playing the shot released a great deal of my nervous tension.

I was delighted with a late cut for 4 in Sohail's next over. People often say I lack a delicate touch against the spinners, so it was a pleasure to play a shot of real finesse. I took an easy single to mid-on next ball. There's almost always a single to either mid-off or mid-on when a spinner is bowling in a one-day game, and I had been on the look out to place the ball there. A spinner cannot afford to have those fielders close enough to prevent the single, for if he does the batsman only has to hit the ball just wide of them to pick up a four.

I enjoy batting with Neil Fairbrother; he's a great nudger of the ball, and a superb judge of a single, which suits my style perfectly, as I need to get a lot of the strike to maintain my rhythm. However, I could sense that he was quite nervous too, and I could feel the pressure increase as the Pakistanis tightened up their bowling and fielding. Neil and I could do no more than take a couple of runs off the next three overs. Ramiz, the acting Pakistani captain in Javed's absence, decided that with four overs left before tea Neil and I were about to close up shop. He brought on Naved Anjum in an attempt to fiddle a few overs before tea, leaving his main strike bowlers with the bulk of the bowling in the last thirty overs. In the circumstances it was the right decision, and he was unlucky not to get away with it. I was aware that if we lost another wicket at this point then the run rate could go up to five an over in next to no time, and I was reminding myself to play myself out of trouble by taking the ones and twos rather than to try to smash the ball to all corners of the ground. However I couldn't resist hitting a leg stump long hop for six over mid-wicket, and when I late cut the next ball fine of third man for four we were back in charge. That over was a turning point; Pakistani heads went down a little, their bowling and fielding lost its edge, and we could comfortably take five an over off the last three overs before tea to maintain the run rate that the openers had set.

In the tea interval I tried to forget about the cricket; I put my feet up, had a sandwich, and called Kath. Shortly before the resumption Goochie had a quiet word urging me to stick it out to the end, and I knew that I would be in trouble with Ian Botham if I didn't because he had already showered and had no intention of taking any further part in the game. Neil and I got straight back into our stride immediately after tea. I'm one of the fastest runners between the wicket in the side, and I always call for a run better with someone like Neil who is as quick as me, rather than with someone like Goochie. In the first over after tea we went through for a couple of extremely sharp singles, and took five off the over without any difficulty.

Waqar was brought back on in a last ditch attempt to pull Pakistan into the game. The usual feelings went through my mind about not wanting to get out to him, but over and above that I knew that if we could play out his spell we would win in a canter. The only thing that was giving me any concern was the weather, as dark clouds were gathering, but there were still too many runs needed for it to affect the way I played. Waqar dismissing Neil in his first over was a real blow. We had already taken four runs off the over, which was more than the asking rate, and we didn't need to force the pace.

With his departure I decided it was up to me to play a more dominant role and allow Allan Lamb time to play himself in. This was a bit of a reversal of roles. Earlier in my England career it had always been Lamby who had nursed me through the early part of my innings, and now I was in a position to return the favour. I was seeing the ball extremely well, and my confidence can be gauged by a shot I played in Anjum's next over. The ball was just short of a length outside the off stump, and there was an easy single to be had by playing the ball off the back foot up to mid-off. Instead I felt aggressive enough to pull high over mid-on for 4.

Lamby was caught behind in Waqar's next over; I thought that this innings might well be Lamby's last international appearance, and I would have loved to have been with him as he bowed out in a blaze of glory. The pressure was now back on, but it was important for me to show no sign of tension. Confidence breeds confidence, so I wanted to remain bubbly, and look as if I was in control for the new batsman.

Graeme Hick was a little on edge when he first came out, and I again aimed to take the initiative by taking most of the strike. This is not quite so easy with Hicky as it is with some batsmen. He isn't a great deflector of the ball, and so he doesn't accumulate many of his runs in singles. He hits the ball so hard that usually it either gets to the fielder too quickly to take a run or goes straight through to the boundary. The good side of batting with Hicky, though, is that once he gets going he scores his runs so quickly that he takes the pressure off his batting partner.

As soon as Hicky came in Mushtaq took over from Anjum, but even his appearance at a crucial time in the game could not shake my confidence. By playing him from the crease he no longer presented a threat; I still could not always pick the googly, but by staying where I was and delaying my shot selection till the last moment I had time to readjust. Despite the loss of two wickets in quick succession we were still scoring freely, and Waqar launched himself for what he must have known was Pakistan's last chance to win the match. He bowled with immense pace, but he must have realized at the end of his next over that it wasn't to be his day. He delivered one hostile bouncer that I saw coming from the moment it left his hand and swayed inside the line. He followed this up with a full length ball on off stump, hoping I would be rooted to the back foot, but I went solidly forward and pushed the ball back up the pitch. I remained in position long after I had played that shot looking up the pitch towards Waqar, letting him know that he had nothing in his repertoire to worry me that day. The next ball was short outside the off stump, and I square cut it for 4, despite the presence of a man out deep on the point boundary.

With my confidence now sky high I felt ready to put my game plan for Mushtaq into operation, and one of the most satisfying moments of the summer was sweeping him for 4 in the next over. When Hicky lofted him over mid-on for 6 later that over, I had no remaining doubts that we would win. Hicky remained relatively impassive after that shot, but I was hopping up and down with excitement. Hicky's nerves seemed to vanish with that shot. I reached my 50 in Waqar's next over. I continued to sweep Mushtaq thereafter, and for the next few overs I was content to take the ones and twos and let Hicky take the bowling apart. He hit Mushtaq for an even bigger 6 over mid-on, pulled Wasim for 4 when he came on in place of Waqar, and the 200 came up in the

37th over.

It began to rain shortly after, and the last thing that I or anyone else in the ground wanted was to have to come back and play out the remaining few overs the next day, and I made an effort to accelerate. I took 9 off Aqib's comeback over, and then Waqar was recalled for his final burst of the summer. All my feelings of not wanting to get out to him resurfaced, and I slapped my side to remind myself to concentrate properly. Regardless of the rain we only needed two runs an over. As if to prove that I could restrain myself, I let Waqar's first ball go harmlessly by outside the off stump, and merely nudged a single off the second. I became more aggressive again after Hicky hit him high over cover for 3, and later that over I cut him over backward point for 4 more. I allowed myself to get carried away by that shot; I launched myself into a cover drive next ball when my feet were nowhere near in position, and I was lucky the shot did not quite carry to the deep cover fielder. I was furious with myself, and I took a few deep breaths to calm down.

The rain was now sheeting down and the umpires offered both sides the chance to come off. We only needed a few runs for victory, and Ramiz had as little hesitation declining the offer as we did. The end was not long in coming. There was just time for Waqar to give me one more bouncer to let me know that he hadn't forgotten me, and for me to reply with a beautifully timed orthodox shot through mid-wicket for 4 to let him know who was boss, before Hicky picked off the winning runs.

I finished on 85 not out, and was delighted to receive my third Man of the Match award of the series. It wasn't a particularly dramatic innings, in that we weren't in crisis when I went out to bat and we went on to win easily, but no international innings is straightforward. I was happy with the way I had met every challenge and had fulfilled my original goal of still being there at the end. All in all, it was the perfect end to a difficult international season.

CHAPTER ELEVEN

THE TOUR

ENGLAND IN INDIA AND SRI LANKA 1993

This was the England tour that most people, myself included, would rather forget; although I ended with some personal success, the Test defeats at the hands of India and Sri Lanka are still painful memories. Yet if there is any truth at all in the saying that you only learn from your mistakes, then the least that can be gained from the tour is a few learning opportunities.

I had injured my toe in a pre-tour net at Lilleshall, but the prospect of missing the first week or so of cricket didn't bother me that much as we flew into Delhi for the start of the tour in late December. Normally I like to get as much practice as I can, both in the nets and in the middle to establish my rhythm, but I was feeling so good about my form that I didn't have the slightest doubt that I would be able to pick up where I left off. Besides, I reasoned that even if I was a little bit rusty when I was passed fit again, there were enough games to get me in good shape for the first Test. As it turned out, I wouldn't have been able to play in the first game at Faridabad even if my toe had mended, because I was sidelined with 'Delhi Belly'.

The tour got off to a difficult start with Graham Gooch's personal problems becoming public knowledge. It must have been a strain for Goochie, and I felt sad for him, but I can honestly say that I didn't detect any less determination or motivation in his approach to this tour as opposed to any other that I have been on with him. He must have had to dig deep at times to maintain his positive attitude, but I don't believe the failure of the tour was related to his captaincy. There's only a certain amount of motivating that a captain can do; after that he has to rely on individuals to turn in the performances. It's too simplistic to say

186

that someone is a good captain if the team does well, and that he's a poor one if it does badly. Team morale only suffered later in the tour, and then only because we kept on losing – and we lost because we played bad cricket. Sure, there were one or two mitigating circumstances, but the fact is that many players didn't perform as well as they could.

What upset me more than anything else in the early days of the tour were reports in the English papers that I wanted to come home. Everyone in the team was concerned about the civil unrest in India. With bombings in Bombay, a curfew in Ahmedabad, and 'shoot-on-sight' elsewhere in the country, it would have been hard not to have been. I happened to make a casual, off the cuff remark to a journalist while we were both taking the same hotel lift, to the effect that if things got worse we should be moved to a safer haven and that if things got really bad then we should come home. It was no more than a statement of the obvious, and yet the next thing I knew was that I was headline news in a Sunday paper and was being quoted as saying I wanted to come home.

To make matters worse, Kathy was then dragged into the story. A local paper phoned her to ask whether she would be happy if I called to tell her that I was coming home the next day. What was she supposed to say? – 'I never want to see him again?' Of course she said yes, and this was twisted to appear in print as 'Kathy's plea: Come Home – Bosses call off Tour'. Before long I was branded the instigator of a players' revolt, and articles appeared saying; 'Grow up or go home Smith', 'One bad egg in the England camp can send jitters through the team with devastating effects'.

The net result was that Kathy was in a state, and I was portrayed as a villain – all because someone wanted to sell a few more papers. I felt that I was manufactured into a mouthpiece for the way everyone was privately thinking, and then made a scapegoat for it. I know that some of the journalists were deeply concerned about the troubles, and they were keener than anyone to come home if the violence escalated. The way the whole affair was reported was without question infinitely more upsetting than the violence itself.

I had a lot to prove in India, both to myself and others, and I wanted the chance to do it. Once the management confirmed that they were in close contact with the British High Commission who were monitoring the situation carefully, I was more than happy to continue with the tour and never gave another thought to my safety.

My first game was against the Board President XI at Lucknow. As soon as I got to the crease I realized that my two week lay off had affected me more than I had imagined. I felt completely out of sorts and it was no surprise when I got out after messing around for half an hour. My form didn't improve in the one-day fixture at Delhi; I was struggling with the slowness of the wickets, my feet weren't moving properly, and one or two doubts began to creep in.

My timing was still out for the first one-day international in Jaipur, but fortunately Alec Stewart was playing superbly and I could take a back seat in our second wicket partnership. The next game at Chandigarh was decided by the toss; the wicket was damp at 8.30 in the morning and the Indians wouldn't have thought twice about putting us in. It was bad luck for us, but in a way it worked to my advantage. We quickly slumped to 49-4 and survival was the order of the day. I had the time to play myself in gently, and it was a big boost to my confidence to post my first respectable score of the tour.

Next stop was Cuttack, and it was here that the team's health started to go downhill. There were two or three players who weren't feeling that well, and they should possibly have kept themselves more to themselves by not coming to the ground; as it was the virus spread rapidly, and there was scarcely a player who wasn't laid low at some stage thereafter. On the field my fortunes continued to improve as I compiled a six and a half hour 149 not out against an Indian Under-25 XI. I had realized that I was never going to take the spinners apart on this tour, so I knew that if I was going to make runs in the series I was going to have to bat for a long time. My concentration was tested to the limit by the heat and the unfamiliar conditions, and I was thrilled by the way I came through.

An overnight train journey to Calcutta wasn't ideal preparation for the first Test, but even so, in the nets before the game began I felt as if I was in the form of my life. We practised on two of the best batting wickets that I've ever played on. They were reasonably fast with a bit of bounce, and Devon Malcolm, Paul Taylor, and Chris Lewis were all charging in. Geoff Boycott was watching from behind to give me a bit of inspiration, and I don't think I have, or ever could, play better. This practice turned out be pointless for both the bowlers and me. The Test wicket was a slow turner, and I didn't face a single ball of pace in either innings.

In hindsight it was a mistake to start the match with just one spinner when India had three in their side, but the wicket did look a little uneven, and we felt that Paul Taylor's extra pace might be useful. Yet to my mind, the match, and indeed the series, turned on Azharuddin's innings of 182. Cricket is often a game of 'if onlys', and if the cut that he played against Ian Salisbury before he was into double figures had gone to hand, instead of just looping over my head at backward point, India might have struggled to reach 200. We would then have been on top, and the Indian spinners may never have had the luxury of bowling with so many men around the bat. Kumble, Raju, and Chauhan, maintained their dominance of that first innings throughout the series, and their bowling was the difference between the two sides.

The England first innings got off to a bad start, and the score was soon 37-2. Within minutes things were even worse as I played around my legs to be caught off bat and pad for 1. It was a poor shot – the result of nervousness and inexperience of the conditions. My plan for Kumble was much the same as it had been for Mushtaq; to play him from the crease and to delay committing myself to a stroke until the last moment. I had been practising this at Lilleshall before the tour began, but none of the practice nets remotely resembled an Indian wicket. You can't really change a quick, bouncy indoor wicket into one that is slow and uneven.

The result was that I learnt the wrong technique; the length at which you decide to play forward or back was completely different in India. If you played back to the same length ball as at Lilleshall, you stood a good chance of being bowled by a ball that went underneath your bat, as Mike Gatting discovered. Therefore if you were in any doubt, you had to play off the front foot. When you couple this with the extra bounce that Kumble could generate and my tendency to lunge at the ball when I'm tense and nervous early in an innings, a bat pad dismissal was always on the cards.

I like to get a Test series off to a good start, and visions of the first Test at Brisbane on the Australian tour of 1990-1 momentarily crossed my mind. However, I'm a great deal tougher mentally now than I was then; I crowded my head with positive thoughts, and was reasonably confident about batting in the second innings. I stayed in for almost an hour, and though I was never comfortable, I felt as if I was coping until I was given out, caught behind off Chauhan. I've talked about luck elsewhere, and this dismissal was another example of not getting a break when it mattered. I don't believe that I ever edged the ball to More, but the umpire didn't agree, and there was nothing I could do about it.

Having gone to Eden Gardens full of confidence, I departed feeling low. England had been convincingly defeated, and I had failed in both innings, which was something of a rarity for me. I wasn't totally unhappy though,. and my morale was quickly restored by runs against the Rest of India at Vishakapatnam. Many critics had written me off after Calcutta, but I was feeling distinctly perky when we arrived in Madras for the second Test. I had decided that I had played with too much humility in the first Test; I had been over respectful to the three spinners, and had allowed them to dictate to me. I was now going to be much more positive; I would still play Kumble from the crease, but I would use my feet against Raju and Chauhan to try to upset their length.

Goochie was too ill to play after his infamous prawn curry the night before, and I was drafted in to open the innings. Fletch and Goochie had discussed this possibility with me before the tour started; they felt that as I was much happier against the seamers I could get the team and myself off to a good start against the new ball, and that by the time the spinners came on I would be comfortably settled with a few runs on the board. I had said that I would be willing to do whatever was in the best interests of the team, although I would still rather bat at 4 if given the choice, and I was now about to find out what I had let myself in for.

We lost the toss for the second time, and had to endure two gruelling days in the heat while India got the best of the Chepauk wicket. By the time they had amassed their total of 560-6 the wicket had begun to turn sharply, and we were always going to be under pressure to save the follow on. Kumble opened the bowling, and I was forced to compromise on my decision to bat positively. A batsman has to be seen to be doing the right thing and going after the bowling from the word go; when you're opening the innings and the side needs 360 to avoid the follow on is definitely not the right thing. You have to balance aggression with playing proper Test match cricket. From a personal point of view I would probably have been better off giving the ball a smack rather than trying to accumulate runs with close fielders surrounding the bat. I stayed at the crease for a long time, but when I was adjudged LBW to Kumble I only had 17 to my name.

Opening the innings was much more straightforward the second time round after we failed to save the follow on. We were so many runs behind that I thought there was nothing to be lost by going for my shots, because I wasn't going to survive that long by pushing the ball around. I got off to a flying start against the medium pace of Prabhakar and Kapil Dev and thereafter I played with aggression and confidence. My 50 came up quite quickly, whereupon I decided to consolidate because I didn't want to throw my wicket away through being too aggressive. This was a mistake; I became tentative once more, and was caught off bat and pad pushing at Kumble. I was disappointed with this dismissal, but if someone had offered me those second innings runs in advance I would have taken them with open arms. I had scored 26 runs in three innings, and to come back like this was an achievement of self-belief, determination, and concentration.

The pressure was now off me, and the tour became psychologically much easier from now on. I had made Test runs, I was beginning to get to grips with the conditions, and, last but not least, Kath was flying out to join me for the Bombay Test. Before I left for India we had agreed that Kath would stay at home, but life on tour had had its ups and downs and we decided to change our minds. My only regret was that Harrison couldn't come too, but it seemed unfair to subject him to the ordeals of the inoculations, flight, and heat, just for one week.

We won the toss and batted at Bombay, though we may have misread the pitch. The ball turned more on the first day than at any other time in the match, and the writing was on the wall when we lost our first 6 wickets for only 118. I was out playing tentatively yet again, getting a thick edge which travelled via several parts of my anatomy to the keeper. My despondency was mitigated by the pleasure of seeing Hicky finally play the way I've always known he can, and chalking up his first Test century in the process. Despite Hicky's brilliant 178, India still made a first innings lead of nearly 250, and our second innings was another rearguard action. Walking out to bat with two wickets having fallen cheaply I felt much the same as I had at the Oval the previous summer. Whatever happened, this was going to be the last time I had to face the Indian spinners on their own wickets. I went out there determined to play a few shots and enjoy myself. With such a positive attitude I scored a second half century to end the series on something of a high note. Even so, I had fallen short of my own high standards. I had said before the tour that I would have been delighted with 250 runs in the series, and satisfied with 200; a total of 146 was well below par.

There were still four one-day games and the Sri Lanka leg to come, but team morale was now low. We kept things together for the first two games, but by the time we reached Gwalior many of the players had had enough. Patience is a necessary virtue in India.

192

Enthusiastic supporters phone you in the middle of the night, or worse still come banging at your door to let you know that you are their favourite cricketer. Breakfast often fails to arrive and you have to go hungry through the first session because there's no food at the ground. Transport is unpredictable, and wherever you go you need an armed guard to keep well-wishers from mobbing you. All these things are bearable when you're winning matches, but when combined with poor results it was no surprise that tempers began to fray. Nevertheless, my personal motivation was still high and it was a good feeling to make my first international hundred abroad, but I suppose it was fitting that Mohammad Azharuddin, the man who had set India on the road to victory in Calcutta, should drive the final nail into our coffin with a peerless one-day innings at Gwalior.

The team tried to raise itself for the games against Sri Lanka. Everyone wanted to salvage something from an unsuccessful tour, but it wasn't to be. We lost the first one-day game, and even though we were given a rest day before the first Test, we were too jaded and tired for it to make much difference. It was nice to score my first Test century overseas a few days later, but in the context of the game I would rather have made a couple of 90s and for England to have won.

Opening the batting in the Colombo Test was one of the most difficult innings I have ever played. The heat was debilitating and concentration was hard to maintain. Mike Atherton went early on, Mike Gatting and Graeme Hick both got out when they looked to be in command, and so the onus was on me to try and hold the innings together. I was thrilled to bat through an entire day for the first time but I was shattered at the end of it, and my dismissal the next morning was simply due to exhaustion. One of the drawbacks of batting for so long was that I had precious little rest before spending a day and a half in the field, and when I committed the basic error of being bowled behind my legs in the second innings it was again because I was too tired to concentrate.

It was a relief to end on a personal high note and take my tally in the four Tests over the 300 mark, thereby maintaining my goal of a minimum of 75 runs per game. Yet any tour with such dismal team results must lead to some serious soul searching by the players. It's not my intention to discuss selection, itinerary, or health because these are matters for others to ponder, and I will limit my thoughts to my own experience.

I believe that I have come back from the sub-continent a better cricketer and a better person. I struggled against the spinners, Kumble in particular, in unfamiliar conditions and while I admit I still have much to learn, I'm proud of the way I battled through. I survived the tour with my confidence intact and with a greater belief in my powers of concentration. I will also take much less for granted from now on. Witnessing so many Indians struggling with poverty, pollution, and poor health, on a daily basis was infinitely depressing, and certainly helped to keep the cricket in perspective. When I spotted Kath and Harrison happy and well in the arrival lounge at Heathrow airport I realized that I had a lot for which to be thankful.

CHAPTER TWELVE

———————

CAREER STATITICS

Smith, Robin Arnold

(Northlands High School), born Durban, South Africa, 13 Sep 1963. Brother of C. L. Smith (Natal, Glamorgan, Hampshire and England 1977/78 to 1991) and grandson of Dr. Vernon L. Shearer (Natal; triple blue for Edinburgh U). 5' 11" tall. RHB, LB Natal 1980/81 to 1984/85. Hampshire debut 1982. Cap 1985. One of *Wisden's* Five Cricketers of the Year for 1989.

Tests: 40 (1988 to 1992-93); HS148* v WI (Lord's) 1991. Limited-Overs Internationals: 55. Tours: Australia 1990-91; West Indies 1989-90; NZ 1991-92; India1992-93; Sri Lanka 1992-93. 1000 f-c runs in a season 6 times; most – 1577 in 1989. HS 209* v Essex (Southend) 1987. BB 2-11 v Surrey (Southampton) 1985.

L-O competitions: match awards: NWT 5; BHC 3. Best performances:

NatWest Trophy:	HS 125* v Surrey (Oval) 1989.
	BB 2-13 v Berks (Southampton) 1985.
Benson & Hedges Cup	HS 155* v Glam (Southampton) 1989.
Sunday League:	HS 131 v Notts (Nottingham) 1989.
	BB 1-0 v Yorks (Leeds) 1992.

OTHER CAREER NOTES

First-class debut 1 January 1981 for Natal B v Transvaal B at Durban when he scored 16 and 15 in a drawn three-day Castle Bowl match.
Hampshire f-c debut 30 June 1982 v Parkistanis at Bournemouth scoring 8 and 1.
County Championship debut on 8 June 1983 scoring 100* v Lancashire at Bournemouth.
Represented Natal Nuffield XI 1978-80 and South African Schools 1979-80.
South African under-17 shot putt champion and Natal Athletics colours 1980.
Hampshire 2nd XI debut 1981.
Played full back for Romsey RFC.

ROBIN SMITH IN ALL FIRST-CLASS MATCHES

Batting and Fielding

	M	I	NO	HS	Runs	Avg	100	50	Ct
England (Tests)	40	74	14	148*	2954	49.23	8	20	29
England XI (on tour)	17	27	7	149*	1149	57.45	2	8	7
MCC (v Worcs 1989)	1	1	-	56	56	56.00	-	1	-
Hampshire (Championship)	134	223	36	209*	8177	43.72	20	36	95
Hampshire (other f-c)	15	25	8	132	1058	62.23	4	4	13
Natal	30	52	5	109	1412	30.04	1	10	12
Totals	237	402	70	209*	14806	44.59	35	79	156

Bowling

	O	M	R	W	Avg	Best
England (Tests)	4	2	6	-	-	-
England XI (on tour)	7	2	27	-	-	-
MCC (v Worcs 1989)						
Hampshire (Championship)	128.1	22	598	11	54.36	2-11
Hampshire (other f-c)	10	3	32	1	32.00	1- 8
Natal	3.5	-	28	-	-	-
Totals	153	29	691	12	57.58	2-11

ROBIN SMITH'S TEST MATCH CAREER

Series	Opponents	Test	Venue	Result	No	Runs	HO
1988	**West Indies**	4	Leeds	L-10w	6	38	c
					5	11	lbw
		5	The Oval	L-8w	4	57	c
					4	0	lbw
1988	**Sri Lanka**		Lord's	W-7w	6	31	b
					5	8	*
1989	**Australia**	1	Leeds	L-210	6	66	lbw
					6	0	c
		2	Lord's	L-6w	6	32	c
					6	96	b
		4	Manchester	L-9w	4	143	c
					4	1	c
		5	Nottingham	L-I+180	4	101	c
					4	26	b
		6	The Oval	D	4	11	b
					4	77	*
1989-90	**West Indies**	1	Kingston	W-9w	5	57	c
					-	-	-
		3	Port-of-Spain	D	5	5	c
					5	2	lbw
		4	Bridgetown	L-164	5	62	b
					7	40	*
		5	St John's	L-I+32	5	12	lbw
					6	8	*(rh)
1990	**New Zealand**	1	Nottingham	D	5	55	c
					-	-	-
		2	Lord's	D	5	64	c
					5	0	hw
		3	Birmingham	W-114	5	19	c
					5	14	c

Series	Opponents	Test	Venue	Result	No	Runs	HO
1990	**India**	1	Lord's	W-247	5	100	*
					5	15	b
		2	Manchester	D	6	121	*
					5	61	*
		3	The Oval	D	7	57	c
					6	7	*
1990-91	**Australia**	1	Brisbane	L-10w	5	7	b
					6	1	c
		2	Melbourne	L-8w	4	30	c
					4	8	c
		3	Sydney	D	4	18	c
					5	10	*
		4	Adelaide	D	4	53	c
					5	10	*
		5	Perth	L-9w	4	58	c
					4	43	lbw
1991	**West Indies**	1	Leeds	W-115	6	54	ro
					6	0	lbw
		2	Lord's	D	6	148	*
					-	-	-
		3	Nottingham	L-9w	6	64	*
					6	15	c
		5	The Oval	W-5w	4	109	lbw
					4	26	c
1991	**Sri Lanka**		Lord's	W-137	4	4	c
					4	63	*
1991-92	**New Zealand**	1	Christchurch	W-I+4	4	96	c
					-	-	-
		2	Auckland	W-168	4	0	c
					4	35	b
		3	Wellington	D	4	6	c
					4	76	c

Series	Opponents	Test	Venue	Result	No	Runs	HO
1992	**Pakistan**	1	Birmingham	D	4	127	lbw
					-	-	-
		2	Lord's	L-2w	4	9	c
					5	8	b
		3	Manchester	D	4	11	lbw
					-	-	-
		4	Leeds	W-6w	3	42	c
					3	0	c
		5	The Oval	L-lOw	4	33	b
					4	84	*
1992-93	**India**	1	Calcutta	L-8w	4	1	c
					4	8	c
		2	Madras	L-l+22	1	17	lbw
					1	56	c
		3	Bombay	L-l+15	4	2	c
					4	62	b
1992-93	**Sri Lanka**		Colombo (SSC)	L-5w	1	128	b
					1	35	b

ANALYSIS OF ROBIN SMITH'S TEST CAREER

Series	Opponents	M	I	No	HS	Runs	Avg	100	50	Ct
1988	West Indies	2	4	-	57	106	26.50	-	1	2
1988	Sri Lanka	1	2	1	31	39	39.00	-	-	-
1989	Australia	5	10	1	143	553	61.44	2	3	1
1989-90	West Indies	4	7	2	62	186	37.20	-	2	2
1990	New Zealand	3	5	-	64	152	30.40	-	2	2
1990	India	3	6	4	121*	361	180.50	2	2	1
1990-91	Australia	5	10	2	58	238	29.75	-	2	3
1991	West Indies	4	7	2	148*	416	83.20	2	2	2
1991	Sri Lanka	1	2	1	63*	67	67.00	-	1	1
1991-92	New Zealand	3	5	-	96	213	42.60	-	2	5
1992	Pakistan	5	8	1	127	314	44.85	1	1	7
1992-93	India	3	6	-	62	146	24.33	-	2	2
1992-93	Sri Lanka	1	2	-	128	163	81.50	1	-	1
	Australia	10	20	3	143	791	46.52	2	5	4
	West Indies	10	18	4	148*	708	50.57	2	5	6
	New Zealand	6	10	-	96	365	36.50	-	4	7
	India	6	12	4	121*	507	63.37	2	4	3
	Pakistan	5	8	1	127	314	44.85	1	1	7
	Sri Lanka	3	6	2	128	269	67.25	1	1	2
Home		24	44	10	148*	2008	59.05	7	12	16
Overseas		16	30	4	128	946	36.38	1	8	13
Totals		40	74	14	148*	2954	49.23	8	20	29

Batting Highlights

Scored hundreds on his first appearance against both India and Pakistan.

Completed 1000 runs in his 14th Test (25th innings) and 2000 runs in his 27th Test (50th innings).

Bowling

Has bowled just one spell (v New Zealand at Christchurch in 1991-92):

O	M	R	W
4	2	6	0

ROBIN SMITH IN LIMITED-OVERS INTERNATIONALS

Batting and Fielding

M	I	No	HS	Runs	Avg	100	50	Ct
55	54	7	129	1886	40.12	3	12	18

Bowling - none.

Hundreds (3)

Score	Opponents	Venue	Series
128	New Zealand	Leeds	1990
103	India	Nottingham	1990
129	India	Gwalior	1992-93

Statistics supplied courtesy of Bill Frindall.